Library of
Davidson College

Liturgical Change:
How Much Do We Need?

with study guide

by Leonel L. Mitchell

A Crossroad Book
The Seabury Press · New York

The Seabury Press
815 Second Avenue
New York, N.Y. 10017

264
m681l

Copyright © 1975 by The Seabury Press, Inc.
Printed in the United States of America

All rights reserved. No part of this book may be reproduced in any form whatsoever, except for brief reviews, without the permission of the publisher.

Quotations from the New Testament, unless otherwise noted, are from *Good News For Modern Man*, copyright © 1966, 1970, 1971 by American Bible Society. Passages from the Psalms are quoted from *The Book of Common Prayer*.

LIBRARY OF CONGRESS CATALOGING IN PUBLICATION DATA

Mitchell, Leonel Lake, 1930–
  Liturgical change, how much do we need?

  "A Crossroad book."
  Bibliography: p.
  1. Liturgics—Study and teaching. I. Title.
  BV176.M57   264   74-26928
  ISBN 0-8164-2113-7

76-8511

Contents

	Introduction	5
I	Change and the Unchangeable	9
II	The Core of Christian Worship	22
III	Contemporary Common Prayer	41
IV	One Use: Uniformity and Diversity	54
V	Praying the Liturgy	69
VI	Go Forth into the World	85
	Leader's Guide for Group Use of *Liturgical Change: How Much Do We Need?*	97
	Books for Further Reading	119

Additional Books Cited in the Background Reading

A three-cassette recording of *Liturgical Change: How Much Do We Need?* is available from Catacomb Cassettes, a Division of the Episcopal Radio and TV Foundation, 15 Sixteenth Street, N.E., Atlanta, Georgia 30309.

Introduction

I have devoted a good portion of my time during the last ten years, both as a parish priest and as a seminary and university professor, to helping people and groups understand why the worship of the Church is changing and how to come to terms with these changes.

The late Dean William Palmer Ladd of the Berkeley Divinity School, where I both studied and taught the liturgy, wrote in 1941:

> Our Book of Common Prayer is the best in the world. For four centuries it has exercised an incalculable influence for good throughout the English-speaking world. To find fault with it is an ungracious task. Yet we must remember that its great virtue is due to the fact that originally it was an adaptation of older services to the needs of its own day. That adaptation was made 390 years ago. Since then the world has changed. Controversies that influenced the old compilers and revisers are now dead. The needs of the twentieth century are not those of the sixteenth. And liturgical science has made enormous progress, even in the last twenty-five years. The time for reconsideration seems ripe
>
> *Prayer Book Interleaves*, p. 107

It is more than thirty years since these words were written, but they have lost none of their cogency. It is in this spirit that I have worked and taught, and in which I offer these pages.

This study guide is designed to help individuals and parish groups to deal with liturgical change. It is not a rationale for, nor defense of, any particular set of proposals for such change, although I would be less than candid if I denied my general support of the proposals of the Standing Liturgical Commission of the Episcopal Church.

Many Christians, and most Episcopalians, react strongly to changes in worship. Some of this is simply a reflection in the liturgical sphere of general attitudes toward change in society, but it is also true that *lex orandi—lex credendi* is an operational principle in Christian theology. In simple language this means that what we believe is both determined by and expressed in what we say and sing in our worship, and the texts of its prayers and hymns are often a truer guide to the actual faith of a Christian community than a study of its theological textbooks. Historically, this has been especially true of the Anglican Church.

Episcopalians are not alone, however, in experiencing liturgical change. Roman Catholics, Lutherans, and many others are experiencing profound changes in their inherited patterns of worship, and they are reacting in the same ambivalent way as Episcopalians. This course, with a small amount of adaptation, should be useful to groups of other Churches, or to ecumenical groups seeking to explore the problem together.

This guide is in two parts. First there are six chapters which are meant to serve as background reading for group discussion. They can be read, hopefully for profit and pleasure, by people who do not take part in a course, but they are written as an integral part of a study plan. Following the six chapters you will find outlines for six group sessions.

Introduction

I should like to acknowledge the many helpful suggestions I received throughout the preparation of this book from the Rev. Reid Isaac, Senior Editor of Crossroad Books. They have in many ways improved it. I am grateful also to the members of my pilot class at the Cathedral of St. James in South Bend where the sessions were tried out.

These pages are dedicated and addressed to the multitude of concerned and confused Church members who are earnestly looking for help in understanding and praying the liturgy of the Church.

LEONEL L. MITCHELL

University of Notre Dame
Pentecost 1974

I
Change and the Unchangeable

Change is the only constant factor in the history of our planet. This is a familiar cliché. But there have been periods in which change was not so apparent as it is today. Marshall McLuhan, the English professor turned communications specialist, assures us that the Western world, which has lasted roughly since the fifth century B.C., is now passing away under the pressure of the new electronic media, chiefly television and the computer. The mere coexistence of "the new electric galaxy of events," he assures us, "brings trauma and shock to every living being." Books such as Toffler's *Future Shock* confirm our fears. The trauma and shock are everywhere evident.

But surely, you may protest, this change does not affect the Church. The gospel is one and unchanging. "Jesus Christ is the same yesterday, today, and for ever" (Heb. 13:8). Christianity is handed down to us from the apostles and the ancient fathers of the Church. How can we even talk about changing it?

There is real point to your protest, and to alter the Faith once delivered to the saints is a most serious matter. St. Paul warns us, "But even if we, or an angel from heaven, should preach to you a gospel that is different from the one we preached to you, may he be condemned to hell!" (Gal. 1:8.) But the world to which we are sent to proclaim Christ is constantly changing, and the gospel needs to be translated into terms which the world can understand. This means more than translating the actual language of the proclamation from Hebrew and Aramaic and Greek into English, Spanish, Swahili, or some other modern language. It means translating its thought into forms which our culture can comprehend, so that the original message shines through undistorted. This is not easy, and opinions will vary as to whether any attempted translation has in fact done so, but this does not excuse us from making the effort. For if we fail to translate the gospel into terms which the world can comprehend, then we fail to bear witness to Christ, and we allow Christianity to become the preserve of antiquarians, with no impact on the modern world.

St. Paul's figure of the Christian life as a race may help us. God is, as he always has been, the start and the finish of the race which we are called upon to run, but the course which we must travel is through the world of the 1970s. This means that our race will not necessarily cover the same ground and may well differ substantially from that of those who ran in another time and place. The practical advice of even the greatest saints may be of little use to us if it is rooted in a culture different from ours. Our goals may well be the same, but the means by which we achieve them may have to be radically different.

Worship in a Changing World

We cannot live in any time but our own, and it would be a serious error to attempt to make our worship real by withdrawing from the present to live ideally in the past. This was precisely the mistake made by the forerunners of the Liturgical Movement who sought to reestablish the worship of an earlier age. Among Roman

Catholics this took the form of recreating, usually in a monastic community, the daily life of the high Middle Ages, so that the Latin Mass and Gregorian chant took on new meaning in a culture similar to that in which it originally developed. Among Anglicans, it was most frequently expressed by the "enrichment" of the worship of the Book of Common Prayer with material from the medieval Sarum Rite, or from the 1549 Prayer Book. The fact that something had been done in another, and presumably better, age was sufficient warrant for its reintroduction today. The wearing of the cassock, gown, and square cap by clergymen on the streets of London in the present century, in accordance with the directions of the English Canons of 1604, is, perhaps, a sufficiently clear example of this tendency.

More recently, and with somewhat greater appropriateness, the worship of the early Church has been held up as a model for modern churches to follow. But it makes little difference whether the "golden age" we seek to recover is the high Middle Ages, the first years of the Reformation, or the apostolic age. We do not live in their world. We cannot live their lives, and we cannot offer their worship. Our worship must be the offering of *our* lives, the only ones we have, to God.

This does not mean that we must abandon our history and construct forms of worship afresh for each age. It does mean that we cannot uncritically accept and continue to use, or revive and introduce into use, forms of another age which do not say what we wish to say, or say it in ways which would either not be understood at all, or be misunderstood in our culture.

In many ways we live in an age of nostalgia in which we retreat from change into the simpler life of an earlier day. The Old West, the '50s, World War II are the substance of a great deal of contemporary entertainment and represent man's continual yearning for "the good old days." But in our romantic reconstructions of the past, we tend to forget what it was really like. As Harvey Cox has forcefully reminded us, "Most of us today would vigorously object to living in the house or doing the job our great-grandfathers did. The fact is that most people's great-grandparents were dirt-poor and lived in hovels." (*The Secular City*, p. 52.)

In the Church, too, we want to see everything the way it was. We picture the church of our childhood, conveniently forgetting its weaknesses, and try to recapture it at its best. But this is a different world. We can no more live in 1928 or 1948 than we can in 1549 or 325. Our present concern is to examine critically the worship of the immediate past. What was appropriate worship when we were children may actually be no more appropriate for our parish today than would the opening service of the Council of Nicea. Most lay people exhibit a healthy skepticism toward the liturgical treasures of the past which enthusiastic priests wish to introduce uncritically into the parish worship, but they are less quick to apply the same critical standards to the forms of worship of their own youth, and to consider whether they are still truly suitable.

Vatican Council II, in launching the Roman Catholic Church on what surely must be one of the most radical liturgical revolutions of all time, laid down some significant general principles. Among them are these:

> The liturgy is made up of immutable elements divinely instituted and of elements subject to change. These not only may but ought to be changed with the passage of time if they have suffered from the intrusion of anything out of harmony with the inner nature of the liturgy or have become unsuited to it.

Change and the Unchangeable

> In this restoration, both texts and rites should be drawn up so that they express more clearly the holy things which they signify; the Christian people, so far as possible, should be enabled to understand them with ease and to take part in them fully, actively, and as befits a community.
>
> Finally, there must be no innovations unless the good of the Church genuinely and certainly requires them; and care must be taken that any new forms adopted should in some way grow organically from forms already existing.
>
> *Constitution on the Sacred Liturgy* 21, 23

The "immutable elements divinely instituted" in Christian worship are few indeed. From Christ himself come the use of Bread and Wine for the Holy Communion, and water for Baptism, and the original text (not the English translation) of the Lord's Prayer. Almost everything else is within the authority of the Church to change.

The Eucharist

In addition to these divinely instituted elements of Christian worship, there are others so universal and, in a proper sense, traditional that their alteration would make a decisive break with the Christian past. A traditional outline for the Eucharist has been followed by most Christians since at least the second century:

1. Readings from Scripture. Following the tradition of the Jewish synagogue, Christians have regularly begun their Sunday Eucharist with readings from the Bible. Among these readings from both Old and New Testaments, the Gospel has the place of honor, traditionally last.

2. Preaching. Not only is the Word of God read in the Christian assembly, it is expounded, and our earliest accounts of the Eucharist outside the New Testament already speak of the presiding minister exhorting the congregation to the imitation of what they have heard in the readings.

3. Common Prayer. Following the sermon, Christians have from the earliest days offered their common prayers for the Church and for the concerns of the Christian community. Often this has been accompanied by the exchange of the kiss of peace, although this has not been universally done.

4. Offertory. Although our Lord took the Bread and Wine separately at the beginning and end of the Last Supper, Christians have traditionally taken both together and placed them, with other offerings, upon the Holy Table.

5. Thanksgiving. Following the example of Christ, we offer thanks over the Bread and Wine "that we, receiving them according to his holy institution, may be partakers of his blessed Body and Blood." This is the chief prayer of the Eucharist, and is the special liturgy, or action, of the presiding minister, who prays it in the name of the congregation.

6. Fraction. The breaking of the bread is practically necessary if we are to share "one loaf." Even when individual wafers have been customary, the solemn Breaking of the Bread, the earliest name of the service, has been retained.

7. Communion. The eating and drinking of the Bread of Life and the Cup of Salvation in obedience to the command of Christ is, of course, one of the central and essential acts of the Eucharist. It frequently gives its name, Holy Communion, to the entire service.

We already find this outline in A.D. 150, in the *First Apology* of Justin Martyr, one of our earliest descriptions of Christian Sunday worship:

Change and the Unchangeable

> On the day called Sunday there is a meeting in one place of those who live in the cities or the country, and the memoirs of the Apostles and the writings of the Prophets are read as long as time permits. When the reader has finished, the president in a discourse urges us and invites us to the imitation of these noble things. Then we all stand up together and offer prayers. And, when we have finished the prayer, bread is brought, and wine and water, and the president similarly sends up prayers and thanksgivings to the best of his ability, and the congregation assents, saying Amen; the distribution of the consecrated elements takes place and they are sent to the absent by the deacons. Those who prosper, and who so wish, contribute, each as much as he chooses to.
>
> *I Apology* 67

When a celebration of the Eucharist is conducted today in accordance with Justin's description, what is most frequently observed is its similarity to contemporary practice. The perseverance of this structure throughout the centuries testifies to the truly traditional character of even the "new" liturgies. Each age and each culture has clothed this traditional material in its own trappings, so that it can speak to the people of God. Few serious suggestions have been made for the abandonment of the basic structure, although attempts have been made from time to time to alter it radically.

The most radical suggestion for the alteration of the traditional form is made by those who propose to substitute other elements for the bread and wine instituted by Christ. It is suggested that bread and wine are too tied to the culture of the Near East, and that the use of coffee and doughnuts, or coke and potato chips, would speak more readily to the present age. Another form of this proposal was made in the nineteenth century by missionaries to China and Japan, who suggested the possible substitution of tea and rice cakes for bread and wine, since neither grapes nor wheat was native to those countries. These suggestions raise in the most profound way the question of when translation becomes alteration of the original message. Many would contend that not only bread and wine, but Jesus himself are tied to the culture of first-century Palestine, and that the elements of bread and wine used by him had a meaning which transends their place, or lack of it, in our culture.

Others have suggested that the "service" format of the Eucharist be abandoned, and the Lord's Supper be celebrated at an actual meal, with the consecration of the Bread before, and that of the Wine after, supper. Some of the more radical groups at the time of the Reformation made similar suggestions, seeking to make the Christian Eucharist a literal representation of the Last Supper.

Evaluating Forms of Worship

The question of the abandonment of traditional liturgy was seriously raised by the distinguished Roman Catholic scholar Romano Guardini in an open letter to the Mainz Liturgical Congress in 1964:

> Is not the liturgical act and, with it, all that goes under the name of "liturgy" so bound up with the historical background—antique or medieval or baroque—that it would be more honest to give it up altogether? Would it not be better to admit that man in this industrial and scientific age, with its new sociological structure, is no longer capable of a liturgical act? And instead of talking of renewal ought we not to consider how best to celebrate the sacred mysteries so that modern man can

grasp their meaning through his own approach to truth?

This seems a hard saying. But there are quite a number of people who think this way.

Herder Correspondence, August 1964, p. 239

For better or worse, the "new" liturgies have answered Guardini's question in the negative, and have followed the Greek liturgies, the Latin Mass, the *Deutsche Messe* of Luther, and the Book of Common Prayer in adapting the traditional liturgical forms. All of these have spoken powerfully to the men of their own times and places, and the contemporary revisers and renewers of the liturgy desire to follow in their footsteps.

Our task is to examine the forms of worship which we have received from the immediate past to see whether they are adequate for our contemporary needs. Do they do what we wish to do? Do they say what we wish to say? If not, how can they be changed to do a better job of presenting the lives of God's people today to him in worship?

The *Constitution on the Sacred Liturgy* of Vatican Council II proposed certain general standards, or criteria, as guidelines for those engaged in the revision of the rite of the Roman Catholic Church:

> The rites should be distinguished by a noble simplicity: they should be short, clear, and unencumbered by useless repetitions; they should be within the people's powers of comprehension, and normally should not require much explanation.
>
> *Constitution on the Sacred Liturgy* 34

Whether the actual reforms introduced into Roman Catholic worship meet these criteria is, naturally, a valuable question for Roman Catholics to discuss. For those of other churches, on the other hand, the Council's criteria are simply suggestions, which we should consider in drawing up our own criteria for contemporary worship.

Whenever we look at the services of worship which have been prepared for our use, we make use of criteria in evaluating them. Often these criteria are not articulated, even to ourselves. We say, "I like this," or "I don't like that," without considering why we have come to that decision. But if we are to carry our discussion beyond the simple level of likes and dislikes we must give some attention to the standards of judgment which we use in reacting to a service of worship. Sometimes we derive our criteria quite consciously from our understanding of the liturgy. We may say that the words or actions are not comprehensible to us, and therefore the liturgy is unsuitable for our use, or that the music is too difficult for the choir to sing, or the sermon too long. Often they are more subjective in nature, or are derived inductively from other experiences which we have found good or bad.

Our criteria may well be quite different from those applied by the compilers of our liturgy. We may judge the worship in which we participate by standards of a different sort from those on the basis of which it was compiled. This is almost inevitably so when we consider a service composed in the sixteenth century, or even earlier. It may also be that the application of the same criteria will result in different evaluations. The English Reformers were concerned that worship be "in a language understanded of the people." We may agree with them that this is important, but still find their English difficult for modern men to understand.

Whatever our criteria are, we make use of them in evaluating the worship in which we participate. It is our criteria which enable us to say why we like this or dislike that. It is important for us to be able to identify the criteria which underlie our reactions to the liturgy if we are to discuss our views with other people.

Here is one set of criteria which you might want to consider adopting for evaluating contemporary worship: clarity, corporateness, flexibility, celebration, and continuity.

1. Clarity. While it is not necessary that everything done in Christian worship be immediately transparent to the chance visitor, it should be clear to the worshiper what he is doing and why he is doing it. Words which are not understood need to be critically examined to see if they should be replaced. Ceremonies and symbols should illuminate the words, not require further explanation.

2. Corporateness. Liturgy is common prayer. It is not intended to be a performance by a priest for an audience. There will certainly be different roles in worship (singer, reader, deacon, communicant) but the priestly people of God must have a part in their worship and not allow it to be usurped by clergy or choirs.

3. Flexibility. The Book of Common Prayer and other sixteenth-century liturgies wished to end the complexity of the medieval services. The preface to the first Book of Common Prayer says that it frequently took longer to find out what to say or sing in the services than to do it. The Prayer Book, for example, solved this problem by eliminating almost all of the variable features of the services. There is no reason today why the same rite need be used for Ash Wednesday in a country parish and Christmas Eve in a great cathedral.

The Methodist liturgist James F. White has written: "Gutenberg made it possible to put prayer books in the hands of the people; A. B. Dick made them obsolete." ("Worship in an Age of Immediacy," in *Christian Century* 75 : 229.) Even if we do not believe the Prayer Book to be obsolete, we are no longer limited by a printed book. Mimeograph and Xerox make it possible to produce "orders of service" for special occasions, either guiding worshipers to other parts of the printed book or supplementing its forms with additional material "proper" to the occasion.

4. *Celebration.* This is a word we have always used about the Holy Communion, but it has not always come through in its performance. The gospel is, after all, good news, and Christian worship is its celebration. This does not mean that we must go through life in a forced cheerfulness, but that we remember that Easter follows Good Friday. Even a funeral celebrates the Resurrection and our continuing fellowship in the Communion of Saints.

5. *Continuity.* New forms should clearly be related to those traditionally used, so that worship is seen to be continuous with that of the Church throughout the centuries. Margaret Mead has said with great appropriateness:

> A good ritual system is like a natural language ... it has to be old, because otherwise it won't have had enough imagination expended on it. It has to be old to be available to everyone born within that tradition. But it must be fresh enough so that it can contain new vision and changed form. This is in a sense, as I understand it, what the liturgical movement is trying to do with the ritual of the church: to use the old symbols, but use them anew, to free them and ourselves from a period of rigidity and stagnation.
>
> *The Ritual Expressions of the Cosmic Sense,* pp. 11f.

Perhaps you disagree with some of these criteria. Probably you wish to adopt others in their place, or in addition to these. But criteria you must have. They are the stan-

Change and the Unchangeable

dards of evaluation you use to explain what you feel to be good or bad in your own worship. Certainly there is room for disagreement as to how well these, or any other criteria we may choose, have been followed in the actual new liturgies now in use or in preparation. Your criteria may differ markedly from those here suggested, but it is against your own criteria that you evaluate the new liturgies. The better you are able to identify your criteria for worship, the better you will be able to explain what you like or dislike about the new liturgy.

What is necessary for us all is to look critically at our forms of worship, both "traditional" and "new," and see how they can be vehicles of our offering of our best to God. What we need today is not a pale copy of Geneva, or Sarum, or renaissance Rome, or even of Nicea or Jerusalem, nor is it an importation into the Church of contemporary secular culture. We must celebrate, rather, our own life in God, and with one another in him.

II
The Core of Christian Worship

"*Worship,*" says Marianne Micks (*The Future Present*, p. ix), "is an active verb. Like *love,* it refers to something people do. People who worship and people who love generally suppose that they know what they are doing." But just as one who is not in love finds the actions of lovers amusing or embarrassing, so too one who does not worship finds it hard to understand why we do the particular things we do when we worship. And when we are asked about it, we find it extraordinarily difficult to explain.

A classic definition of worship is that given by Evelyn Underhill:

> Worship, in all its grades and kinds, is the response of the creature to the Eternal: nor need we limit this definition to the human sphere.
>
> *Worship,* p. 3

This definition suggests that worship is a perfectly natural activity, and one in which man joins with the rest of the created universe. It sets our human actions in a larger framework of what we might call cosmic worship. This is an idea which is frequently expressed in Scripture. Psalm 19, for example, begins, "The heavens declare the glory of God; and the firmament showeth his handiwork." The same theme is expressed again in Psalm 148:

The Core of Christian Worship

> Praise the Lord from the heavens:
> > praise him in the heights! . . .
> Praise him, sun and moon:
> > praise him, all ye stars and light. . . .
> Let them praise the name of the Lord:
> > for he spake the word and they were made;
> > he commanded and they were created.

Most Episcopalians are familiar with its expression in the canticle *Benedicite,* the "Song of the Three Young Men," which is used at Morning Prayer. In *Authorized Services 1973* it is entitled "A Song of Creation." It begins by calling upon all the works of the Lord to "praise him and magnify him for ever" and, after an extensive listing of the works of the Lord, calls upon men to join in this universal chorus of praise:

> O ye children of men, bless ye the Lord:
> > praise him and magnify him for ever.

St. Francis of Assisi also gave his voice to this chorus in his "Canticle of the Sun" (Hymn 307, *The Hymnal 1940*), in which he calls upon brother sun, sister moon, mother earth, sister water, brother fire, and even sister death to join with all creation in the praise of the Creator. In a somewhat different way in our own century the scientist-theologian Teilhard de Chardin has expressed this idea in his *Hymn of the Universe.*

Man's Place in Worship

In this universal chorus of praise, humans have a unique place, for we alone join it by choice. The heavens cannot help but proclaim the glory of God. It is by their very existence that all other creatures praise God. We must decide whether or not to join our voices to their chorus, for we can refuse to offer our praise to God. Or to look at it positively, humanity alone in creation is able freely to respond to God, to return God's blessing with its own, to put into words the prayer of the universe in which the Psalmist, St. Francis, Evelyn Underhill, Teilhard de Chardin, and a host of others have called upon all to join.

By this action of giving voice to the response of all creation to their God, we act as a kind of priest, a priest of nature. The Russian Orthodox theologian Alexander Schmemann expresses human priestly activity in this way:

> He stands in the center of the world and unifies it in his act of blessing God, of both receiving the world from God and offering it to God—and by filling the world with this eucharist, he transforms life, the one that he receives from the world, into life in God, into communion.
>
> *For the Life of the World,* p. 5

This is a description of natural religion. We receive the things of the world from God and offer them back to God in thanksgiving. "All things come of thee, O Lord, and of thine own have we given thee" (I Chron. 29:14). The Greek word *eucharist* means "thanksgiving," and in offering thanks to God for what we receive, we are making eucharist. Fr. Schmemann's point is that when we do this we are united with the world and its Creator in a natural communion. All of us have had at least hints of this natural communion with God in nature in the pure joy of ex-

The Core of Christian Worship

periencing good and beautiful things, but most of us lack the words to express it. Teilhard de Chardin, in "The Mass on the World," wrote:

> All the things in this world to which this day will bring increase; all those that will diminish; all those too that will die: all of them, Lord, I try to gather into my arms, so as to hold them out to you in offering. This is the material of my sacrifice; the only material you desire.
>
> Recieve, O Lord, this all-embracing host which your whole creation, moved by your magnetism, offers you at the dawn of a new day.... In the very depths of this formless mass you have implanted—and this I am sure of, for I sense it—a desire, irresistible, hallowing, which makes us cry out, believer and unbeliever alike: "Lord, make us *one*."
>
> *Hymn of the Universe,* p. 20

"The Renegade Priest"

But, in point of fact, we have not fulfilled our natural priesthood. We have been unthankful to God, unloving, and uneucharistic. The contemporary Anglican theologian Robert Capon has well described us as "the renegade priest." We have refused the priestly role in which God has cast us. In the words of Dean Capon:

> The sins by which man has ruined the shape of the world are precisely the acts of a spoiled priest: resentment, prejudice, envy, hate, lust, greed, sloth, pride. Sin is not accidental or irrelevant: it is the oblation of the right things in the wrong way.
>
> *An Offering of Uncles,* p. 66

Sin has rendered us unable as well as unwilling to worship God naturally. We are fallen, alienated from God. But the gospel of Jesus Christ proclaims God's mighty act in the face of this alientation. God has restored our priesthood in the person of Jesus Christ his Son. The Word became flesh and dwelt among us; Christ was made the high priest of a New Covenant, the head of a new and redeemed humanity, the reconciler of God and man, the Saviour of all creation. The worship which we were unable to offer naturally, we can now offer "through Jesus Christ our Lord."

Christian worship is first and always "through Jesus Christ," for in him we experience the fullness of divine priesthood uniting us with God in perfect praise, thanksgiving, and self-offering. The *Constitution on the Sacred Liturgy* describes corporate worship as "an exercise of the priestly office of Jesus Christ . . . an action of Christ the priest and of his body which is the Church" (par. 7). It is the offering of the new human race, of which Christ is the head and only true priest, and in which he binds us to himself and to each other by the power of his Holy Spirit as members of his body. This is why the Church has traditionally offered its common prayer to the Father, through Jesus Christ, in the fellowship (or communion) of the Holy Spirit. It is so much a corporate act that even when the Christian prays alone he is taught to say, *"Our* Father," for in the act of praying we are united with one another in Christ and the Spirit.

Worship in Early Centuries

Many scholars believe that the worship of the early Church consisted only in the celebration of the two sacraments of Baptism and Holy Communion. Baptism unites us with Christ in the mystery of his death and rising again.

The Core of Christian Worship

> By our baptism, then, we were buried with him and shared his death, in order that, just as Christ was raised from death by the glorious power of the Father, so also we might live a new life.
>
> Romans 6:4

Holy Communion proclaims and renews our unity in that mystery until it is manifested in his "coming again in glory to judge the living and the dead."

> For until the Lord comes, you proclaim his death whenever you eat this bread and drink from this cup.
>
> I Corinthians 11:26

Whatever was true of the first generation of Christians, we do know that by the middle of the second century Christians had adopted as their Sunday worship a service compounded of prayer and Scripture reading similiar to that of the Jewish synagogue, and the taking, blessing, breaking, and giving of Bread and Wine following the command of Christ at the Last Supper. This service was described in the second century by St. Justin Martyr in the passage quoted in the first chapter. It is the basis of all traditional Christian liturgies, including those of the Book of Common Prayer, the Roman Missal, the Lutheran Service Book and Hymnal, the Book of Common Order, and so forth. An outline of it is given in the first chapter.

This traditional outline is divided into the Liturgy of the Word and the Liturgy of the Sacrament (or Eucharist). They represent the two principal aspects of Christian worship. The heart of the Liturgy of the Word is the reading and exposition of the Bible to the people of God. It is the proclamation of God's Word to his people. Everything else in this part of the service is intended to enhance that proclamation: beautiful music, solemn processions, powerful preaching. All are focused upon the opening of the Word to the people.

From the earliest days the response of the people to this proclamation has been intercessory prayer. Justin Martyr wrote: "Then we all stand up together and offer prayers." What did they pray for? Justin mentions that they pray for themselves "and all others everywhere, that we may be made worthy, having learned the truth, to be found good citizens and keepers of what is commanded, so that we may be saved with eternal salvation." (*I Apology* 65.) An extensive litany of intercessions for this purpose has survived from the fourth century in the document called *Apostolic Constitutions*. The Prayer for the Whole State of Christ's Church, in the Book of Common Prayer, is a sixteenth-century example of such a prayer.

Intercessory Prayer

Certainly the prayers of Christian people are an important part of public worship. Even when a Liturgy of the Word is held without the Liturgy of the Sacrament following, prayers and intercessions are integral parts of the service. But we can hardly expect the content of the prayers to remain constant throughout the centuries. In the Middle Ages and in the Reformation era when the world and Christendom were thought of as co-terminous and kings were believed to rule by divine right, a prayer such as this would come naturally to Englishmen:

> We beseech thee also to save and defend all Christian Kings, Princes, and Governors, and specially thy servant Edward our King, that under him we may be Godly and quietly governed: and grant to his whole

The Core of Christian Worship

council, and to all that be put in authority under him, that they may truly and indifferently administer justice, to the punishment of wickedness and vice, and the maintenance of God's true religion and virtue.

Second Prayer Book of Edward VI, 1552

Certainly the least of our problems with this petition today is the change in meaning of the English word "indifferently." Should we not pray also for non-Christian rulers? Justin had no hesitation in praying for a pagan and persecuting emperor, nor did St. Paul. Do we believe that the function of civil government is to punish wickedness and vice, and to maintain the true religion?

Or does this really say what we want to say?

> We beseech thee also, to rule the hearts of those who bear the authority of government in this and every land [especially _____], and to lead them to wise decisions and right actions for the welfare of mankind, and for the peace of the world.

Authorized Services 1973, p. 36

These petitions embody different concepts of the function of civil government. The vast majority of Christians today understand the relationship of the state not only to the Church, but to its own citizens and to the world community, very differently from the way they were understood in the sixteenth and seventeenth centuries, and *our* prayers should say what *we* mean.

An example more central to Christian belief of the change in attitude which separates most modern Christians from those of an earlier age is found in this prayer for the sick:

> Almighty, everlasting God, Maker of all mankind who dost correct those whom thou dost love, and chastise every one whom thou dost receive; we beseech thee to have mercy upon this thy servant visited with thine hand, and to grant that he may take his sickness patiently. . . .
>
> Book of Common Prayer, p. 321

Do we really want to say that? In point of fact the prayer is seldom used, but it expresses a particular view of sickness as a punishment sent by God. This idea has its roots in Hebrews 12:5, which is provided by the Prayer Book as a Scripture reading to follow the prayer we have quoted:

> My son, despise not thou the chastening of the Lord, nor faint when thou art rebuked of him: for whom the Lord loveth he chasteneth, and scourgeth every son whom he receiveth.
>
> Book of Common Prayer, Epistle for Communion of the Sick

There is, on the other hand, a New Testament tradition attributed to Jesus himself in the Gospels which sees sickness not as the work of God, but as an effect of evil against which Christ contended throughout his life in his healing miracles, and over which he triumphed in his rising from the dead. Most pastors would prefer to follow this line in

The Core of Christian Worship

ministering to the sick, and the alternative prayer added to the Prayer Book in 1928 which prays for healing is almost always used.

Quite apart from the extremely dubious notion that those who are sick are being punished by God, the entire gloomy tone of the prayer, which probably reflects fairly accurately the medical situation of the sixteenth century, is hardly likely to inspire confidence in the sick person to whom the Church is seeking to minister in the name of Christ. Unfortunately, a great many prayers for the sick composed in this century are so cheerful in tone that they seem to refuse to take seriously the possibility that the sick person might die.

Perhaps more than any other part of our worship, common prayers of intercession need to be regularly revised, not only so that they do not say the wrong thing, but so that they actually do pray for the needs and concerns of the contemporary Church. One new intercession, for example, prays for those who travel through outer space. Whether or not we like the particular petition, it at least expresses a concern which the Church could not have had before now.

The new Roman Catholic liturgy has allowed the leaders of prayer almost complete freedom to construct their own Prayers of the Faithful for each specific occasion. This gives unlimited flexibility, but leaves the way open for lack of imagination and poor style. The Book of Common Prayer provides a single unchangeable Prayer for the Church (p. 74). *Services for Trial Use* provides seven alternative Prayers of Intercession in a variety of styles. This attempts to steer a middle ground between rigidity and total flexibility, but many people complain that they cannot find the intercessions in the book, and instead of praying they spend their time frustratedly flipping pages. This complaint is particularly important when those intercessions which do not have a uniform response are used. If the congregation's part is an unchanging "Lord, have mercy," or "Lord, hear our prayer," it is possible to listen and respond without following the petitions in the book, but if (as in Intercessions III and VII) the congregation responds differently to each bidding, it is important that everyone be able to find the words. Many parishes have attempted to deal with this problem by printing booklets containing the service *as they use it*, with most of the options omitted. Only one or two Prayers of Intercession are usually included. We must answer the question, "How much flexibility do we want?" but we need also to ask, "How much can we handle?"

The "Kiss of Peace"

Anciently the common prayers of the faithful concluded with the exchange of the "kiss of peace," a sign of our union and communion with one another in Christ. Among Western Christians it died out during the Middle Ages, except in monasteries, but was revived in the mid-twentieth-century by the Liturgy of the Church of South India, in the form of a double hand-clasp. From there it has spread to both Protestants and Catholics, or more properly, it has inspired them to revive it in their own traditions, either at the close of the prayers or before the reception of Communion. For many people this recovery is the high spot of the Liturgical Movement. It is a moving, almost sacramental, expression of our oneness in Christ. For others it is a serious affront, an interruption of their prayer, a meaningless triviality, or an acute embarrassment.

Liturgical piety stemming from the Middle Ages, but reinforced by the Reformation, Counter-Reformation, and Pietistic movements, has tended to focus attention vertically on the relationship between God and the individual believer, to the neglect of the horizontal dimension of unity among the worshipers. The demand to greet your neighbor with the kiss of peace flies in the face of this tradition. It compels us to recognize that we are not alone in the Church with God, but are one of a community. It also goes against many of our cultural conditionings. We are told to keep our hands to ourselves, and never to speak to strangers, from the time we are children. It is hardly surprising that many find it embarrassing to be expected to do so in church.

The peace presents another practical problem in most American churches. The congregation is usually confined in pews, and it is almost impossible to greet anyone other than those seated next to you, often your own family. As one irate churchgoer complained, "I didn't come to church to shake hands with my wife." Some people undoubtedly wish to be left alone with God during the service. Either through shyness, or through conviction, they wish to ignore their fellow communicants, but the peace does not permit them to do this. They quite naturally react with embarrassment and resentment. The peace is a powerful act of nonverbal communication. The question which individuals and congregations must face is, "What does it communicate?"

The Liturgy of the Sacrament

The Liturgy of the Sacrament consists of four actions and a prayer. The actions are offertory, consecration, fraction, and communion. The prayer is the Great Thanksgiving. It is also known as the Prayer of Consecration, the Canon, or the Eucharistic Prayer. It is the central prayer of the Christian liturgy, praising God, through Jesus Christ, in the Holy Spirit.

A great deal of attention has been paid in the past quarter century to the four actions of the Eucharist. Offertory processions have been carefully planned to make clear that the bread and wine, as well as the money, are the offerings of the people. In some places people have baked the bread and made the wine for the Eucharist, and brought them forward to be offered at the offertory. In other places ushers have brought traditional breadboxes and cruets from the back of the church. Sometimes other things symbolic of the people, or of groups within the parish, are brought forward and placed on the altar.

The theological principle behind this new emphasis on the offertory is man's offering of his life and all creation to God through Jesus Christ, in the only way in which it can be offered, in union with Christ's perfect offering of himself. As one group promoting the Liturgical Movement expresses it:

> From the altar, God's redeeming and renewing power reaches out into every phase of life: to the altar every aspect of our existence is to be gathered up and offered to God through Christ in the fellowship of His Spirit.
>
> *Parish Program for Liturgy and Mission*,
> Associated Parishes, 1963

On the other hand, this "offertory theology" has been strongly attacked. We can, its opponents remind us, offer nothing at all to God. We can only come with empty hands and hearts to receive from him. There is certainly a tendency in some places to emphasize the offertory so strongly that it gives the impression that our offering to God, whether of money or of the work of our hands, is the significant act, not the unique self-offering of Christ. This impression can be conveyed as readily by a phalanx of morning-coated ushers bringing alms basins to the altar to the accompaniment of organ fanfares as by the offering of the tools of their trade by workmen and artists in overalls and smocks. Some have even suggested that the offering of bread and wine is more suitable to a pagan fertility cult than to the Christian Eucharist.

Certainly any suggestion that our offerings are in any way to be compared with the sacrifice of Christ is to be avoided. The only spirit in which we can offer anything as Christians is that of the Byzantine Liturgy, which says:

> We offer you your own, from what is your own,
> in all and for the sake of all.

This echoes the familiar words of I Chronicles 19:14: "All things come of thee, O Lord, and of thine own have we given thee."

On the other hand, there can be little doubt that one of the bad effects of the Middle Ages upon Christian worship, a legacy inherited by both Catholics and Protestants, was its clericalization: the restriction of both words and actions to the priest or minister, and possibly an "altar boy" vested to look sufficiently clerical. If offertory processions make clear to the people of God that *they* are participants in worship, not an audience, then they are worth the trouble. If they do not, then at best they are a distracting side-show, and at worst a perversion of the meaning of offering.

The Book of Common Prayer places the offertory before the Prayer for the Church; almost all other liturgies place it immediately before the Prayer of the Great Thanksgiving, so as not to interrupt the action: offering, blessing, breaking, giving. This allows the four actions of the liturgy which we perform, following the example of Christ at the Last Supper, to form a single unbroken action.

The Great Thanksgiving, recited by the presiding priest in the name of the congregation, is the central prayer of the liturgy. At the time of the Reformation it was a serious bone of contention. Luther eliminated it entirely from his mass. Everyone desired to follow the pattern of the early Church, but no one knew what that pattern was. The Canon, the fixed eucharistic prayer of the Latin Church, was well known. The Anaphora of St. John Chrysostom, one of the eucharistic prayers of the Eastern Church, had only just appeared in print in Latin translation, and the eucharistic prayers of the early Church were totally unknown. Today we are much better informed about the nature of the early eucharistic prayer, but there is still much we do not know, and probably will never know.

Justin Martyr tells us simply that the president of the brethren "sends up praise and glory to the Father of the universe through the name of the Son and of the Holy Spirit, and offers thanks at some length that we have been deemed worthy to receive these things from him." (*I Apology* 65.) It seems clear from the earliest texts which we do possess that there was no fixed prayer, but that the celebrant gave thanks "to the best of his ability," improvising on a fixed outline. This outline underlies all of the later fixed texts:

1. Thanksgiving to God, first for creation, and then for redemption through Jesus Christ.

2. Narrative of the Institution of the Eucharist concludes the enumeration of the mighty acts of God in

Christ for which we give thanks, e.g., "We thank you, God . . . for the life and death and resurrection of Jesus Christ, who on the night in which he was betrayed took bread, etc."

3. Anamnesis, or memorial, follows from the narrative of the institution, i.e., "Remembering what Christ did, and following his command, we now offer and present you this Bread and Cup."

4. Invocation, or epiclesis, calls upon God to send down his Holy Spirit to bless and sanctify the Bread and Cup we offer in Christ's name, and to bless the assembled people.

5. Doxology, an ascription of praise to the Father, through the Son, in the fellowship of the Holy Spirit, brings the prayer to a close on the note of praise and thanksgiving with which it opened.

Other elements are sometimes added, such as intercessions, or thanksgivings for specific things, as in the traditional "proper prefaces." But this is the basic outline of eucharistic prayers.

For many centuries the Latin Church used a single invariable eucharistic prayer, the Canon of the Mass. This was the basis of the Prayer of Consecration in the first Book of Common Prayer. The Eastern Orthodox liturgies have always used alternative eucharistic prayers, much as we alter collects and "proper prefaces." The new Roman Catholic Mass provides four alternative eucharistic prayers, and many additional alternatives are widely used. *Services for Trial Use* and *Authorized Services 1973* include a number of alternative eucharistic prayers. Some are versions of the sixteenth-century Prayer Book prayer, others are new compositions. All conform to the same basic structure. Three are provided in traditional language for the "First Service," three in contemporary language for the "Second Service," and three more are included for use with the "Third Order."*

We may ask the same questions about the Great Thanksgiving which we asked about the common prayers of the faithful. Do they say what we wish to say in the way we we wish to say it? Should we invariably use the same prayer, or should there be alternatives? If there are alternatives, will the people be able to find them in the book? Do they need to follow the prayer, or can they pray with the priest without reading the text? How much freedom should the individual priest or the congregation have to alter this central prayer?

The remainder of the Liturgy of the Sacrament is action. The "one bread" is broken so that many can partake, and the consecrated Gifts are distributed to the people of God.

There is increased interest today in eating the "one bread" and drinking the "one cup." The use of individual "wafers" not readily identifiable to sight or taste as "real bread" has become as great a cause of concern to some as the use of individual glasses in place of the "one cup" has been in the past. There is no theological reason not to use substantial bread which can be broken and tasted, and many find it better fulfills the symbolic function of the sacrament. There are, of course, many practical difficulties in the Communion of large numbers from one bread and one cup, and some form of practical compromise is usually worked out.

For Roman Catholics the restoration of Communion under both species has been one of the effects of Vatican Council II. Communion from the chalice was specifically

*The General Convention of 1973 authorized the use of Eucharistic Prayer C (*Services for Trial Use*, p. 84) with the Second Service, giving the 3–3–3 distribution mentioned. The change is included in the rubrics of *Authorized Services 1973*, p. 70.

The Core of Christian Worship

permitted by the *Constitution on the Sacred Liturgy* (par. 55) "when the bishops think fit." The number of occasions upon which it takes place has increased rapidly, and it is seen as a more perfect manifestation of the sacred sign. Here too there are practical difficulties when large numbers are to receive, problems with which Anglicans and Lutherans have contended for four hundred years. Unfortunately, no one seems to have found a perfect solution, preserving the full symbolism, yet easy and not too time-consuming.

Traditionally Episcopalians, Roman Catholics, Lutherans, and Methodists have received the Holy Communion kneeling. Today there is considerable interest in receiving it standing, as in the Eastern Orthodox churches. Both postures have a long and honorable history in Christian practice. Kneeling seems to emphasize the unworthiness of man to approach the Lord, and standing the confidence with which we draw near in Christ.

Noneucharistic Services of Worship

In this chapter we have not discussed the structure of Baptism, nor of special occasions of worship, such as weddings and funerals. We may certainly ask questions about these rites similar to those we have asked about the Eucharist. Do they say what we wish to say? Do they provide enough flexibility, or too much? We must mention, however, the Daily Offices of Morning and Evening Prayer. They have their roots in the praise of God at the beginning and ending of the day, and in the dedication of every day and time to the Lord who "makes the light and creates the darkness," through Jesus Christ, who is the world's true Light. Their focus is on the praise of God in the words of the scriptural psalms and canticles. The offices conclude with prayers of intercession, which are the common prayers of the Church. In the Anglican tradition they include two readings from Scripture and therefore represent a different form of Word liturgy. When this structure is enlarged by a sermon expounding the Scripture it becomes parallel to the Liturgy of the Word in the Eucharist. Over the years the two services have tended to borrow elements from each other, until today they are often seen as alternatives, or even rivals. Both are used as noneucharistic services, and both are used in combination with the Liturgy of the Sacrament.

III
Contemporary Common Prayer

Once we have agreed about the structure of our common prayer, and about what we want to say in it, we are still faced with the formidable problem of saying it. Traditional prayers often contain forms of expression and images which come to the lips of modern congregations only with difficulty.

Collect Form of Prayer

The Latin Liturgy developed a compact style of prayer known as the collect form. Its chief characteristic is that its says much in little, making literal translation into English awkward, if not impossible in many cases. The work of Thomas Cranmer, the chief author of the first Book of Common Prayer, in rendering these Latin collects into forceful English prose for the 1549 Prayer Book remains one of the great achievements of English literature. They strike us as fresh expressions, not as translations. His collect for Ash Wednesday is a good example:

> Almighty and everlasting God, who hatest nothing that thou hast made, and dost forgive the sins of all those who are penitent; Create and make in us new and contrite hearts, that we, worthily lamenting our sins and

acknowledging our wretchedness, may obtain of thee,
the God of all mercy, perfect remission and forgiveness;
through Jesus Christ our Lord.

Until the last decade almost everyone who wrote prayers in English tried to sound like Cranmer, sometimes quite successfully. Cranmer's English, with the occasional emendation of an obsolete word, can be understood for the most part with a little effort by modern Christians, but it is not our vernacular. We do not speak the English of Cranmer anymore than we speak that of Shakespeare, and attempts to compose new prayers in it are often disastrous. But even if we can succeed in composing a prayer for astronauts in sixteenth-century English, do we really wish to do so?

The collect assigned to the Second Sunday after Christmas Day in *Services for Trial Use* is a translation of the first Christmas collect from the sixth-century Leonine Sacramentary:

> O God, who hast wonderfully created us in the dignity of thine own image, and hast yet more wondrously restored us after the likeness of thy Son Jesus Christ: Make us worthy, we beseech thee, to partake of his divine life, who for our sake came to share our human nature.

The Provisional Sacramentary of the Roman Catholic Church handles the prayer this way:

> Lord God,
> we praise you for creating man,
> and still more for restoring him in Christ.
> Your Son shared our weakness:
> may we share his glory.

Both of these versions were written in this century. The Roman Catholic form retains the directness of the Latin by drastically simplifying the structure, making it into two English sentences, and eliminating its references to the two natures of Christ. The Anglican form has kept the structure of the Latin, with its dependent clauses, and has expanded the phrases to make the meaning clear. They represent two different ways of dealing with the same material. The pithy, compound, complex sentences which are the glory of Latin prose style are not common in contemporary English, and many listeners find them difficult to follow and understand.

In most collects the invocation of God is followed by a relative clause: "O God, who makest us glad by . . . , grant that. . . ." Our ears have become accustomed to this cadence. But contemporary English has abandoned the use of the second-person-singular "thou-thee" forms, and the use of the plural forms after *who* sounds strange to most ears: "O God, who make [*not* makes] us glad . . . ," or "Lamb of God, who take away the sin of the world. . . ." The attempt to remedy this situation by inserting the pronoun *you* has caused congregations to dissolve in laughter as God is addressed as "you-who." Sometimes the problem can be avoided by slightly recasting the sentence. The collect "Of the Reign of Christ" (*Services for Trial Use*, p. 620) begins:

> Almighty and everlasting God, who didst will to restore all things in thy well-beloved Son, the King of kings. . . .

The contemporary-language version begins:

Almighty and everlasting God, whose will it is to restore all things in your well-beloved Son, the King of kings....

Another attempt is to recast the thoughts in parallel sentences. This may have the undesirable effect of giving the appearance of informing God, rather than praying. An example of this treatment is this rendering of the Collect for Purity:

> O Lord, we cannot hide from you or deceive you. If our worship of you is to be pure, you must make it so. Cleanse our hearts, breathe your own life and truth deep within us, so that in both word and action our worship may be worthy of you.
>
> Stevick, *Language in Worship,* p. 126

Cranmer's original is this:

> Almighty God, unto whom all hearts be open, and all desires known, and from whom no secrets are hid: cleanse the thoughts of our hearts, by the inspiration of thy Holy Spirit: that we may perfectly love thee, and worthily magnify thy holy name: through Christ our Lord.

It may be difficult, but it is not impossible to write good prayers in contemporary English. It involves more than simply the avoidance of archaic words, however. It requires a simple, direct prose style free from undue complexity.

New Models of Prayer

One way to try to do this is to develop new models of prayer. Models provided in private prayer, such as Malcolm Boyd's *Are You Running with Me, Jesus?* or Michel Quoist's *Prayers,* can sometimes be used effectively in common prayer. Three such prayers by Huib Oosterhuis are provided in the Burial of the Dead in *Services for Trial Use.* This is the first:

> Lord God, you were happy to give us
> the light of our eyes
> and let us be born.
> You did not make us
> for darkness and death,
> but so that we should, with all our hearts,
> live and come closer to you.
> Be merciful to us then
> and take us by the hand
> and lead us to life
> today and forever.

Some would suggest that the abandonment of set forms of prayer for the freedom of extempore prayer is the proper solution. There is indeed much to be said for permitting freedom in prayer, but it does not solve the problem. It simply transfers the problem from the compilers of the liturgy to the individual worshiper, who must still find words that his fellows will understand in which to express his prayer. Anyone who has ever tried to pray aloud extempore will recognize the extent to which his ability to articulate the prayer of his heart is dependent upon his having models of prayer in mind which he can imitate and adapt.

Litanies

The litany form as a model for contemporary prayer has been used extensively. It permits a leader to articulate the subjects for prayer and the people to respond vocally, completing the petition:

> For all who have commended themselves to our prayers: for our families, friends, and neighbors; that being freed from anxiety, they may live in joy, peace, and health, we pray to you, O Lord.
> *Lord, have mercy.*
>
> Intercession V, *Services for Trial Use*, p. 103

This form has the advantage of permitting flexibility of petition, as long as the "cue" for the congregational response remains constant. Whatever the leader says, the congregation, in the form quoted, knows it will conclude "we pray to you, O Lord," to which they reply, "Lord, have mercy." Many people feel that the verbal participation of the congregation in the prayer makes it a better vehicle for common prayer than a long "pastoral prayer" to which they listen in silence and respond only inwardly. Few today will take seriously the Puritan objection to litanies that the alternation of voices is more like the bouncing of a tennis ball than Christian prayer. Nevertheless, many modern litanies fail. It would be hard to fault the intention of the petition of the 1967 Liturgy of the Lord's Supper, "For those who farm the fields and tend the woods," yet the image of wood-tending was widely criticized and ridiculed.

Contemporary Common Prayer

Ways of Addressing God

If we are to compose new prayers in contemporary English, what do we do with those which we already have? Some will argue for a total uniformity of style. Everything must be written in contemporary English. Others will wish to keep traditional forms, mixing them with new prayers cast in a different idiom. For many people the conflict of language will focus on the use of the archaic second-person-singular forms to address God. In the sixteenth century "thou" and "thee" were the regular forms by which one addressed another person. "You" was a plural form. The intent of the Prayer Book was to speak to God in contemporary speech, so that it might be understood by the ordinary man. The men of the sixteenth century who called God "thou" used the same word to address their neighbor, their wife, or their dog. Today the singular form has completely disappeared, and to employ it in prayer is to use a form which serves almost no other purpose.

Many people will defend the continued use of "thou" in addressing God. The evidence of the sixteenth century, they say, is irrelevant. In the twentieth century we have a four-hundred-year tradition of addressing God as "thou" in formal, public prayer, and often in private prayer as well. This tradition may have its roots in the Book of Common Prayer and the King James Bible, but it is the common heritage of all English-speaking Christians, Catholic and Protestant, and to abandon it now would signify the abandonment of the religion, if not indeed the God, of our fathers. Even though "thou" is no longer used in ordinary conversation, it is clearly understood by everyone. The fact that it is reserved almost exclusively for prayer serves to mark prayer as a special undertaking, for which we use a more formal language. It signifies the uniqueness of God and the importance of public prayer.

For others the use of an archaic term of address is evidence that God is not a part of twentieth-century life. If he is not dead, he is at least obsolete, and speaking to him at all is a bit of romantic nostalgia. The use of sixteenth-century language implies that Christianity has never really come to terms with the present and seeks to return to an earlier "age of faith" symbolized by the use of "thou" and "thee." Modern man, they contend, must be able to address God in modern speech, if he is to speak to God at all.

Actually the address of God as "thou" or "you" is only a part of the problem of contemporary prayer. Custom is a powerful conservative, and unless presented with overwhelming reasons to change, man tends to do what he is used to doing. We must, nonetheless, make sure, on the one hand, that we do not throw away the faith of our fathers along with their modes of expressing it and, on the other hand, that we do not continue to say things we do not mean because we are used to saying them in that way. Daniel Stevick, in his *Language in Worship*, has asked the question most pointedly:

> Have we by a dated language, dated the Christian reality? A style is inseparable from a mentality. Does a sixteenth-century English liturgical-language-style suggest inevitably sixteenth-century thought and values? If translation is needed must it not be a translation both of words and of the associated mentality? These are serious questions. The style of prayer is the style of inner religious life. Anyone who says "mere words" might as well say "mere faith." (pp. 149–150)

Images of God as Reflected in Worship Forms

It is Professor Stevick's contention that the Book of Common Prayer does reflect the thought-forms of the royal court of sixteenth-century England, while many of the prayers of the Latin and Greek liturgies reflect their belief in the Christian Roman empire. "O Lord, our heavenly Father, the high and mighty ruler of the Universe, who dost from thy throne behold all the dwellers upon earth" evoked a real image of a royal court when it was written in 1547. It seems strange today as the beginning of a prayer for the President of the United States, although it is provided for that purpose in the American Prayer Book (p. 17). Not only does the language seem inappropriate, but it raises serious questions about both our image of the presidency and our image of God.

The image of God as a monarch enthroned on high, with subjects standing humbly before the throne as suppliants presenting petitions, is one which would come naturally to mind in an age of absolute monarchs, from Constantine to Louis XIV. It is written into many of our prayers, but the image may not be immediately available to moderns. For us a king and a kingdom suggest either "once upon a time" or constitutional monarchies such as England and Sweden. Absolute monarchs we almost automatically consider tyrants or dictators. None of these conveys the picture intended.

If we examine the words of our worship more closely we shall find a great many images, both of God and of the world, which do not correspond to either our experience or our understanding. This tends to produce what Dr. Stevick calls a "credibility gap between what the liturgy is saying and where people are living." The Arab Christian who is called upon to sing "Blessed be the Lord God of Israel!" experiences this gap in its most acute form.

A less acute example is the problem presented by a phrase such as, "Blessed art thou that beholdest the depths, and dwellest between the cherubim." What are we to understand by it? Changing it, as *Services for Trial Use* does, to "Throned upon Cherubim, plumbing the depths, you are blessed and adored," does not really solve the problem. It is, of course, possible to teach people the meaning of the statement, explaining the ancient cosmology which lies behind the "depths" and the significance of the two cherubim *(cherubim* being the Hebrew plural of cherub) who stretched their wings over the mercy-seat of the Temple at Jerusalem where God was said ritually to be enthroned. But when we have done this, have we invested the phrase with any real meaning for people today?

Unquestionably there are some images and figures which are so much a part of the gospel proclamation that it is impossible to do without them. It would be hard to proclaim the authentic gospel without speaking of God as Father. How can we avoid speaking of the Kingdom of God? or the Good Shepherd? But we must recognize that even such basic images do not convey immediate understanding to many people. When, referring to our Lord, we use the scriptural title "High Priest," it is apt to convey the idea that Jesus was a sort of clergyman, which is certainly not what the author of the Epistle to the Hebrews had in mind. We can hardly avoid speaking of Jesus as Christ, but what does Christ mean? For most people it is simply a proper name. Its meaning as anointed king and priest, as Messiah, is lost, and each of those terms we have just used to explain *Christ* will itself require explanation.

Contemporary Common Prayer

Prayers for Contemporary Use

To be true to itself a contemporary prayer must be true both to the gospel and to the world for which we pray. We must speak the truth, but we must speak it in the language of today about the world of today. This is easier to prescribe than to do. Modern prayers often avoid saying the wrong things by saying nothing at all. Some are so general as to become nothing but pious platitudes, while others are so specific that they exclude large areas of human life and many members of the worshiping congregation. To quote Dr. Stevick again:

> Liturgical renewers do not need to consult ancient sacramentaries so much as they need to listen to what is being said by those whose faith has engaged them with the dilemmas of modern society. We need to try to formulate the situation of man today as prayer. We need prayers which communicate the sense of terror and despair of those who care deeply that—with so much against him—man be able to be truly man. We need prayers which communicate also the faith which endures—often, indeed, joyfully—in the midst of terror and despair.
>
> *Language in Worship*, p. 88

Writing prayers for contemporary use is not easy. We have need of theologians who are poets, and of poets who are theologians. Both appear to be in short supply. Simple intelligibilty is not enough. Prayers must have "soul," they must be prayable. They must be able to take their place in the magnificent tradition which is our heritage. English-speaking people are used to excellence in the language of their common prayer and they will not be content with inferior workmanship. In the words of an English Roman Catholic writer:

> If Cranmer were still in purgatory . . . the worst of his pains would surely be the knowledge of how atrociously the Roman Catholics of today have translated the prayers which he once translated so sublimely.
>
> Robert Speight, "Liturgy and Language," in *Theology* 74 (1971) : 456

There is little doubt that many Anglican attempts are no better. The following prayer for relevance was submitted, one hopes in jest, to the Liturgical Commission:

> O God our ultimate concern, who is more likely down than out, and who reveals the void of his being more clearly in our questions than in our answers: Teach us to communicate relevantly with each other across the sacred-secular dichotomy of our existential predicament. Establish authentic I-Thou relationships in the ambiguous context of our pluralistic society. Sensitize us to the hidden agenda of our peer groups in terms of meaningful ego-satisfactions. And help us to confront all disturbed and disadvantaged persons with underlying concern for the paradoxical reality of their interpersonal dynamics. In the name of our mutual responsibility and interdependence in the body of Christ. Amen.

Few modern prayers are as bad as this one strives to be, but many of its faults are found in serious compositions. Modern jargon is substituted for old-fashioned concepts. Paragraphs are used when a sentence would suffice. A simple idea becomes needlessly complex. Fr. Aidan Kavanagh, O.S.B., who quoted the preceding prayer in an article, "A Relevant Liturgy" (*The Way* 11 [1970] : 83), provided a succinct distillation of the thought concealed beneath the mountains of contemporary clichés:

> Fill us with love, compassion, and mercy; through Jesus Christ, in the unity of the holy Spirit in the holy Church. Amen.

This is a model of both contemporary and classical prayer.

Often when we attempt to modernize sixteenth-century prayers by tinkering with their wording, we succeed only in blunting their forceful prose into incredible blandness. "If the salt have lost his savour, wherewith shall it be salted?" (Matt. 5:13) in the King James Bible becomes, "If the salt has lost its taste, how shall its saltness be restored?" in the Revised Standard Version.

Where do we draw the line? When does a word or a phrase need replacement? Abraham Lincoln probably did not often call the number eighty "four score," but he did it with great effectiveness in the Gettysburg Address. What images are essential to the gospel and must be retained, even if they present difficulties? How can we strip off the outmoded clothing of another age and clothe our worship afresh in contemporary garments? These are basic questions, and they do not admit of simple answers. The words of our worship may be modern or classical, but they must not be old-fashioned. The task of writing contemporary common prayers is in a real sense both necessary and impossible, and there will be many views as to how well any specific attempt has succeeded.

IV
One Use: Uniformity and Diversity

When Johann Gutenberg printed the first book from movable type in the mid-fifteenth century he heralded a new day for Christian worship. The printed book, unlike its manuscript predecessor, is exactly like every other book printed from the same type. Books were the first uniform commodity, and their introduction made uniformity in worship completely possible for the first time.

As long as service books were copied by hand each one was custom-made for its prospective owner. When a parish copied the books of the cathedral or of some distinguished church, it usually altered the book to conform to the local usages. Parishes and dioceses developed local uses, or variations of the accepted liturgy. Now printed books could be produced in quantity and their use enforced on different congregations.

In 1549, barely a hundred years after the invention of printing, the first Book of Common Prayer proclaimed boldly in its preface:

> By this order, the curates shall need none other books for their public service, but this book and the Bible. ... And where heretofore, there hath been great diversity in saying and singing in churches within this realm: some following Salisbury use, some Herford use, some the use of Bangor, some of York, and some of Lincoln:

One Use: Uniformity and Diversity

Now from henceforth, all the whole realm shall have the same use.

The medieval diversity of uses was to be ended by the establishment of a single printed book, to be enforced throughout England. To the present day the Book of Common Prayer of the Church of England prints immediately following its table of contents "An Act of Uniformity" dating from 1559, which requires the exclusive use of the liturgy of the Prayer Book in every parish church, cathedral, and other place of worship in England and Wales.

But this was not a peculiarity of the Church of England. In 1570, following the Council of Trent, the Roman Missal of Pius V made its appearance, and the Papal Bull printed in the book itself imposed it upon the Roman Catholic Church throughout the world, to be used without addition or alteration. In the words of the distinguished Roman Catholic scholar Joseph Jungmann:

> The greatest and most consequential innovation of the Mass book of Pius V was the enactment, clearly expressed in its Bull of introduction, that this book was to be, from then on, the standard in every church and that no changes were to be made therein.
>
> *Mass of the Roman Rite* I : 138

For the past four hundred years the ideal of liturgical uniformity has been put forward by both Roman Catholic and Anglican churches. In the American Episcopal Church a national adaptation of the Book of Common Prayer was set forth by the General Convention of 1789. In the Ratification, printed on page iv of the present revision of the Prayer Book, "... they declare it to be the Liturgy of this Church: And require that it be received as such by all the members of the same." The use of the Prayer Book is also enjoined by Article X of the Constitution, and violation of the rubrics of the Book of Common Prayer is set forth in the Canons as one of the charges which may be brought against an ordained minister.

In the Roman Catholic Church the uniformity guaranteed by the worldwide use of the Latin language and the Roman Missal was augmented and reinforced by the establishment in 1588 of the Sacred Congregation of Rites, which provided a uniform interpretation of the rubrics, or directions of the liturgical books, and ruled definitively on any matter not covered by them. In this way Roman Catholic worship acquired the almost total uniformity of which it was accustomed to boast. "Wherever I go, in whatever part of the world, I shall be at home, for the Mass will be performed in exactly the same way."

Liturgical Variations Today and Yesterday

The liturgical changes resulting from Vatican Council II have sharply altered this position. The *Constitution on the Sacred Liturgy* speaks of "legitimate variations and adaptations to different groups, regions, and peoples," and of the necessity for "an even more radical adaptation" of the liturgy in certain places. Not only have the liturgical books issued from Rome since Vatican Council II been adapted by national authorities to conform to the customs and traditions of the country in which they are to be used, but there is great variety, even within the same parish, in the manner in which the rites are performed. One Mass may be solemnly celebrated with traditional ceremonial, choral music, and organ accompani-

One Use: Uniformity and Diversity

ment, while the next is informally done in "mod" style with guitars, balloons, and prayers composed by the priest himself or a parish liturgy committee.

Even when the official texts are meticulously followed, the rites themselves provide such a wide variety of options that a good deal of advance planning by the liturgy team is required. Little but the outline of the liturgy, the order in which the various parts are put together, seems to be unchanging.

Episcopalians have been engaged since 1967 in the "trial use" of various new services. Their situation is somewhat different from that of their Roman Catholic neighbors, for their "old liturgy" has not been suppressed. The 1928 Book of Common Prayer remains in full force as the official liturgy of the church. It is, of course, in the process of revision, but the formal authorization of a new Prayer Book as a total replacement for the present book cannot be earlier than 1979. This is a day for which many Episcopalians yearn with devout anticipation. Some await this day because they see it as the adoption of a "new" order in the church, one they feel is long overdue. Others await simply the end of "trial use." They look for liturgical stability and an end to change.

Both are probably doomed to disappointment. Predicting the future is always risky, but there does not seem to be any strong sentiment for a radical new start in worship, nor for a return to a single order of service, to be used without variation, except in the Scripture readings, week after week. If we can judge the shape of the future by *Services for Trial Use,* the "Green Book" issued in 1970, or *Authorized Services 1973,* its younger brother, there will be greater flexibility both in the words of the liturgy and in the manner of its performance.

Episcopalians are already familiar with a good deal of variety in the way in which the services of the Prayer

Book are conducted. Almost every Episcopalian has at some time attended another parish in which the old familiar services did not seem all that familiar. The words were the same, but the vestments, the music, and the ceremonial of both priest and congregation were different, and he has remarked to himself, or his neighbor, "My, it's very high/low!" There have been periods in which serious attempts were made to require every congregation to use the services of the church in exactly the same way, and "high" and "low" churchmen have fought over crucifixes and candles, Anglican Chant or Plainsong, and whether alb and chasuble or surplice and stole were the "correct" vestments. The only truly positive effect of what were often bitter disputes has been that Episcopalians are aware, in a most practical way, that substantial differences in the details of our worship are possible within the same church. The inconvenience to the visitor from another parish is usually seen as taking second place to the desirability of allowing those who hold a common faith to express their worship in different ways.

It is probably this fact of Anglican history which makes Prayer Book revision so important, and so controversial for Episcopalians. The use of a common liturgy has been seen as the cement holding the Anglican Communion together, and attempts to alter the words of our worship seem to threaten the very foundations of the church.

Actually the first break in the use of a single Book of Common Prayer was the adoption in 1789 of the first American Prayer Book. Today each national or regional church of the Anglican Communion has its own local version of the Book of Common Prayer, and almost all are in the process of revising them. In many countries a local version of the Prayer Book has been used side by side with that of the Church of England for decades (in Scotland for three hundred years), and many Prayer Books contain

One Use: Uniformity and Diversity

more than one order for the celebration of the Eucharist.

In 1967 the authorization of *The Liturgy of the Lord's Supper (Prayer Book Studies 17)* for "trial use" presented American Episcopalians for the first time with an authorized alternative to the eucharistic liturgy of the Book of Common Prayer. In 1970 the present "trial liturgies" made their appearance, providing three alternative orders for the celebration of the Eucharist, and within each order a variety of options. In addition to a revision of the Prayer for the Whole State of Christ's Church, seven alternative intercessions were provided, and in *Authorized Services 1973* even more flexibility was provided by the insertion of a rubric (on p. 83) which reads:

> The forms of intercession which follow may be adapted, provided that prayer is always offered for the intentions listed.

Alternative forms of general confession are provided, and permission is given to use them in various places in the service. Even, or perhaps especially, the Great Thanksgiving, the eucharistic prayer, is provided in eight different versions, including one (Eucharistic Prayer D) which allows the priest to give thanks in his own words in the first part of the prayer.

The "First Service" is a revision of the traditional liturgy of the Book of Common Prayer. The "Second Service" follows the same structure, but uses modern English throughout, and provides three alternative eucharistic prayers which are contemporary compositions. The "Third Order" is actually titled "An Order for Celebrating the Holy Eucharist" and is simply an outline which the celebration must follow "on occasions other than the principal service on Sundays and other Feasts of our Lord."

In a real sense Episcopalians have been embarrassed by a multitude of riches. Many loyal churchpeople see the unity of the church being destroyed by a liturgical smorgasbord. A few see the changes as reflecting radical novelties in theology. Most simply complain that they cannot find their place. Years of practice have made them familiar with the Book of Common Prayer, which any non-Episcopalian will recognize as difficult to follow, and the change of familiar page numbers casts them adrift in a sea of ever changing options, with no certain landmarks.

It must be honestly faced that any form of change is a practical nuisance, but if the change is for the better, we are, by and large, willing to pay the price. We put up with the inconvenience of having our living room repainted, or of moving to a new house, because we expect the result to be worth the trouble. Liturgical change is an important problem for many people, particularly for those who have difficulty reading the new books and have committed the old service to memory. Seventeenth-century Anglicans, many of whom could not read, were attached to the psalms of the "old version" of the Great Bible. This resulted in the Anglican Church never adopting the "new version" of the King James Bible and continuing into the twentieth century to print the old Psalter in the Prayer Book and to use it in its worship. The comments of the preface to the Prayer Book of 1549 still speak to the situation today:

> And if any would judge this way more painful, because that all things must be read upon the book, whereas before, by the reason of so often repetition, they could say many things by heart: if those men will weigh their labour, with the profit in knowledge which daily they shall obtain by reading upon the book, they will not refuse the pain, in consideration of the great profit that shall ensue thereof.

One Use: Uniformity and Diversity

The spirit in which the "trial liturgies" of the Episcopal Church were produced is clearly expressed in the introduction to *Prayer Book Studies 17:*

> The present age is one of liturgical change and experiment. . . . We believe that new experiments and trial usages will in the long run help us to establish patterns of worship more meaningful to the modern age, and give us a flexibility in the present ferment of liturgical renewal.

How Much Change and Flexibility?

The question really is not will there be liturgical change, but what kind of liturgical change will there be. Shall we rearrange our ecclesiastical furniture, put a fresh coat of paint on the wall, and move back in? Or, while we have our liturgical house torn up, shall we make major renovations, replace our worn-out Victorian furniture with modern pieces, and have our priceless antiques refurbished, restored, and placed in a setting which will show them off to their best advantage? Shall we adopt a "new" liturgy and impose it with a new act of uniformity on all and sundry? Or do we wish to retain a wide variety of options for the forseeable future? Should Latin and sixteenth-century English be relegated to the archives? Or do they still have a place in public worship?

Granted that some flexibility is essential in a service book, how much flexibility should there be? Lack of flexibility makes for aridity and narrowness of devotion. It fails to take advantage of the available richness of suitable material and, more significantly, fails to take account of human nature. Variety, we say, is the spice of life. However excellent the play or the dinner, we would not wish to repeat it over and over. Because I prefer Shakespeare and chicken, must I deny my neighbor Beckett and hamburg? On the other hand, too much flexibility destroys all sense of familiarity. I literally never know where I am or what is expected of me. I cannot sing, because I do not know the music. I cannot pray, because my mind is not at peace. In the words of Marshall McLuhan, "Our most ordinary and conventional attitudes seem suddenly twisted into gargoyles and grotesques." (*The Gutenburg Galaxy*, p. 279.)

The churchman who a few years ago unhesitatingly responded, "And with thy spirit," to the traditional greeting of "The Lord be with you," is often unsure today whether to say that, or "And also with you," or perhaps, "And with your spirit." The mere suggestion that we recite the Apostles' Creed is apt to send him flipping through unfamiliar pages to find the present wording of the affirmation he learned as a child. Granted these phenomena are temporary, they may nonetheless be profoundly disturbing and disruptive of prayer. There are liturgical forms that we can and should say by heart and in which we do not want flexibility and variation.

In practice, the person who participates in daily services is likely to want a good deal of variation in the service, lest a deadening monotony quench the fervor of devotion. He or she is apt to be quite familiar with both the service and the service book, and turning to page 76 for alternative Eucharistic Prayer C presents neither practical nor spiritual problems. The full use of various alternatives may, in fact, tap new springs of devotion.

On the other hand, people who attend the Eucharist twice a month or less, are apt to feel confused and resentful of variation. They look for stability and familiarity in the rite as aids to devotion. They are less likely to find the repetition of the same prayers monotonous, because so

One Use: Uniformity and Diversity

much has happened since the words were last used. The familiar words are welcomed as symbols of returning and rest, old friends which help to express the prayers of the heart.

One approach to the question of how much flexibility is desirable is to maintain a rigidity of structure while permitting a total flexibility of form. In other words, the outline of the service, the agenda, what happens next, remains unchanged, while the elements which flesh out the structure admit of considerable variation.

This is the universal arrangement of the "Proclamation of the Word of God." The salutation of the priest introduces a variable prayer (the Collect of the Day). It is a different prayer for every Sunday and feast, but its position in the service is fixed, and it ends with a standard formula which enables the people to respond "Amen." Following the collect are variable readings from the Bible, either two or three in number. The passages are even more variable than the collects, since most of the new lectionaries provide a three-year cycle for the Sunday readings, as well as various alternatives for weekdays. But the order of the readings is always the same. If there is an Old Testament reading, it comes first. If there are three readings, the Epistle follows. Finally, the Gospel is read in last place, and everyone stands for its proclamation. Between the readings, various psalms, canticles, or hymns may be sung or read. The variety in the content, in the words, of this part of the service is almost unlimited, but the structure is totally fixed. Some items may be omitted part or all of the time. There may be no Old Testament lesson, or no Epistle, or no song between the readings, but the clarity of the order of service keeps confusion to a minimum, and there are few who would want us always to read the same Scripture lessons, or always to sing the same hymns or psalms.

The same principle may be extended to other parts of the service, such as the penitential rite, the prayers of intercession, and the Eucharistic Prayer. Probably the use of alternative eucharistic prayers is least confusing to the congregation. As long as the opening dialogue, "Lift up your hearts," is the same, and the "cues" before the Sanctus and the Amen remain unchanged, the use of Proper Prefaces or alternative prayers need not confuse people. Their part remains the same. On the other hand, since the Eucharistic Prayer, or Great Thanksgiving, is the central prayer of the service, which the priest says as president of the assembly at prayer, people are justly suspicious of alterations in the familiar words. They need to be assured that the new prayer means the same as the old, that liturgical revision has not been a smokescreen for theological change. For this reason, writing your own eucharistic prayer is a particularly difficult undertaking.

There are many possible things which can be said in a eucharistic prayer, but any prayer which said them all would be much longer than any presently in use. Proper prefaces, which provide forceful statements of different aspects of Christian doctrine, have formed a part of this prayer in the Western Church for over a thousand years. As with the various biblical readings, the proper prefaces by their variety provide a comprehensiveness which would be difficult to attain in a single prayer of reasonable length. The provision of alternative prayers extends this same principle.

One particular problem for Episcopalians at the present time is precisely that the congregational parts of the liturgy are not always the same. The "First Service" makes use of the traditional language in the responses: "And with thy Spirit; It is meet and right so to do," while the "Second Service" uses the modern forms: "And also with you; It is right to give him thanks and praise." There

One Use: Uniformity and Diversity

are also different versions of the Gloria in Excelsis, the Creed, the Sanctus, and the Lord's Prayer.

The obvious question is: Why don't they make up their minds? The answer is not always satisfactory. The modern translations are those of the International Consultation on English Texts (ICET), which is ecumenical as well as international, and has the thoroughly praiseworthy goal of providing the English-speaking world with common forms for those prayers which Christians have in common, so that wherever we are, in Australia, England, or Swaziland, and in whatever Christian church we are worshiping, the wording of these common forms will be identical. Unfortunately the effect has been, at least temporarily, quite the opposite. It has provided a new set of English forms which now compete with those previously in use. Perhaps this is a temporary phenomenon, and the ICET texts will be universally adopted, or discarded. But, in the interim, it is a real source of confusion. The contemporary language services of American Episcopalians, Roman Catholics, and Lutherans use the ICET texts, with a good deal of hedging about using the new text of the "Our Father," while the older Anglican and Lutheran services retain the traditional forms. In the case of the creeds this confusion was felt by the Standing Liturgical Commission of the Episcopal Church to be intolerable, and the ICET texts of the creeds are used throughout *Services for Trial Use* and *Authorized Services 1973*, except for the retention of the older version of the Apostles' Creed in the "First Service" Burial of the Dead, on p. 376 of *Services for Trial Use*.

There seems to be good reason to retain the forms hallowed by four hundred years or more of continuous use when traditional language is used, and also to be good reason to adopt the common translations of English-speaking Christians, if indeed the ICET texts can become that. We shall have to decide whether the positive values of retaining both outweigh the inevitable confusion.

Roman Catholics have made the decision to use twentieth-century English in the liturgy. They have had no tradition of liturgical English to hold them back, and have moved boldly, perhaps recklessly, into the use of contemporary idiom. They do, nevertheless, use the familiar form of the "Our Father" in the mass, rather than the ICET text, which occurs in other services. For much the same reasons, many Episcopalians and Lutherans are unwilling to abandon the forms with which they are familiar, and retain and use "traditional language" services along with newer versions. The Standing Liturgical Commission of the Episcopal Church has provided for the Eucharist, Morning and Evening Prayer, and the Burial of the Dead a "First Service" which retains the traditional language of the sixteenth century, with some revision. The structure of the Eucharist is the same in both the traditional "First Service" and the contemporary "Second Service," but the words which are used are different. In some cases they are modernizations of the older prayers, in others they are new compositions.

To abandon the "First Services" would seem to many Episcopalians to be cutting themselves off from their own past, to be rejecting a substantial part of their own history. Loyalty to the Book of Common Prayer seems to preclude abandoning its traditional formulations. But to refuse to speak modern English in the liturgy would be to abandon the very principle of vernacular worship which produced the Book of Common Prayer in the first place. If we therefore provide, as seems to be the case, both options as alternatives, we must be prepared to live with a certain amount of confusion. Perhaps some compromise could be made, so that the most common responses, such as the

One Use: Uniformity and Diversity

answer to "The Lord be with you," could be always the same. It would certainly help to reduce the feeling of confusion most people experience when they are uncertain which set of responses they should give.

As long as the principle of "one use" is accepted by the Church, then all of these questions must be given a single answer. A three-year cycle of readings causes no problem, as long as the whole church uses it in the same way. But as soon as we permit St. Peter's to use service A, while St. Paul's uses service B, the principle has been abandoned. If within the same parish we find a contemporary service for the Family Eucharist, a traditional order at a later hour for the more conservative members, and a free-form "Third Rite" liturgy in the evening to "turn on" those who are alienated from traditional "church," we find that a new principle of liturgical adaptation has replaced it.

Many people believe that the principle of liturgical uniformity, of "one use," is indeed dead, and should be given decent and speedy burial. A plurality of uses, they feel, best expresses the worship of our multiform society. It matters little whether the diversity is between parishes, or within the same parish. People are different, and need to worship in different ways, if their worship is to be an authentic offering of themselves to God in Christ. One contemporary scholar phrased it this way:

> Hopefully the Church will begin to see that the outline, not the prose style, is the real backbone of the rite. Furthermore, this outline is the same in the revised Roman Mass, in the revised Lutheran and Presbyterian services, and in other recent revisions. . . .
>
> Indeed, when this traditional Christian liturgical outline is followed, you don't really need a prayer book at

all. If you simply listen and watch, you will know just what is happening.

H. Boone Porter, Jr.,
Worship in Spirit and Truth, p. 14

How willing is the Church to allow congregations, or groups within congregations, or even dioceses to establish their own pattern of worship within the traditional Christian liturgical outline? Some groups wish to continue to try everything, to make every Sunday new and different, but most find a rite that suits them and wish to use only a limited number of optional variations from it.

The unity of the Church obviously requires some continuity from congregation to congregation, and the mobility of modern society makes it a practical necessity. Christians must be able to move freely from place to place and enter into the worship of different congregations as communicating members, not as visiting strangers. Dr. Porter has suggested in the passage quoted above that the use throughout the Church of a single "traditional Christian liturgical outline" will be sufficient. Others will want more uniformity, but how much? Shall we remain in the era of the paperback liturgy, or can the variety of present-day worship really be contained within the covers of a book? A book which contains all possible options would be too confusing to use for many people. Others would find one which did not include them an unbearably rigid straitjacket. Certainly the greater the diversity permitted, the clearer must be the common core of our worship which binds us all together as One Bread, One Body.

V
Praying the Liturgy

> At the heart of it all is the Eucharistic action, a thing of an absolute simplicity—the taking, blessing, breaking and giving of bread and the taking, blessing and giving of a cup of wine and water, as these were first done with their new meaning by a young Jew before and after supper with His friends on the night before He died. ... He had told His friends to do this henceforward with the new meaning "for the *anamnesis* [recalling]" of Him, and they have done it always since.
>
> G. Dix, *The Shape of the Liturgy*, pp. 743–744

These words of Gregory Dix, probably the best-known Anglican liturgical scholar of this century, go right to the heart of the matter and point out what is so obvious that it is often overlooked. The Eucharist, the Lord's Supper, the Holy Communion, the Mass, is that simple. Common, everyday foods are blessed and distributed, eaten and drunk, in fulfillment of the command of Jesus Christ who said that to eat this Bread and to drink this Cup was to participate in the mystery of his death and resurrection—to enter into the life of the new age.

Christian worship derives historically from Jewish worship, in which the tradition of the sacred meal, eaten by the family in the home on the Sabbath and at Passover, stands at the heart of religious practice. This is the tradition in which Jesus and the apostles grew up, and it is the tradition in which they met together in the Upper Room for what we call the Last Supper. There is in this tradition an explicit recognition that eating and drinking are themselves sacred acts. Bishop Arthur Vogel, in his book *Is the Last Supper Finished?* quotes approvingly the words of Fr. Louis Bouyer:

> A common meal makes men appreciate their relation with the cosmos which provides the natural resources for their life. Eating in common is the human act *par excellence,* where society is built up as from within, while each man perfects himself by integrating himself with the universe.
>
> Quoted from Bouyer, *Rite and Man,* p. 90

A meal, by itself and without the need of anything else, is full of sacred meaning. It brings man face to face with the sacredness of life—including his own life—for the preservation of which animals are killed and crops harvested. It makes us aware of our total dependence on the God who feeds and preserves his people. On Thanksgiving Day, for example, we give thanks to God, not just by saying grace but by eating a meal with our family and friends. It is the eating, as much as the praying over it, which makes Thanksgiving Day a celebration.

The Thanksgiving dinner also illustrates another aspect of the eucharistic meal. It is not a solitary act. "Come on over for dinner!" is what we say to someone we wish to know better. Eating together is more than just an expression of friendship; it is, in a real sense, one of its causes. By including other people in our family group at the dinner table we enter into a new relationship with them.

Praying the Liturgy

Whenever we wish to celebrate ritually our relationship with others we do it with food or drink. The hamburg and coke after a movie, the champagne and cake at a wedding reception, the cup of coffee we offer a friend who stops in to see us—all express and tend toward increasing our oneness. At a wedding, a funeral, a business conference, or in the casual meeting of friends, food is the natural accompaniment of conversation, an expression of unity achieved or desired. As Fr. Alexander Schmemann expresses it:

> Centuries of secularism have failed to transform eating into something strictly utilitarian. Food is still treated with reverence. A meal is still a rite—the last "natural sacrament" of family and friendship, of life that is more than "eating" and "drinking."
>
> *For the Life of the World*, p. 5

The point of all this is that Jesus did not simply find the Last Supper a convenient time to institute a new ritual and seize upon bread and wine as its symbols because they happened to be readily at hand. There is in the act of eating and drinking itself a natural element of worship, a sacredness which was explicitly recognized by the Jewish tradition of which Jesus and the Twelve were part. So when our Lord instituted the Holy Eucharist at a meal he did not act arbitrarily, but out of a religious tradition inherent in the nature of things, and out of the specific historic tradition of Judaism.

The two significant religious moments of the Jewish sacred meal come at the beginning and at the end. At the beginning of the meal, bread is broken and distributed to all the participants with the blessing, "Blessed art thou, O Lord our God, King of the Universe, who bringest forth bread from the earth." And at the end a great blessing, thanking God for the meal and all his blessings, is pronounced over a cup of wine, which is then drunk by all. It was these two ritual actions upon which Jesus conferred a new meaning at the Last Supper, and which Christians repeat in the Holy Eucharist, for his Memorial.

Unity of God and Man

Whatever else the Eucharist is, and it is many things, it is a celebration of man's oneness with God and with his fellow men, a unity which Jesus himself brings into being. In Chapter II we spoke of man's unique place in the worship which all creation offers to the Creator, and of his failure to fulfill his priestly role. The gospel message is that Jesus Christ did not fail, but perfectly fulfilled his Great High Priesthood. In his life and death and rising again, he did perfectly what man is called to do, uniting men and all creation to God in and through himself. In our union and communion in him in his Body, the Church, he gives us a share in his priestly work. "Christians," says Bishop Vogel, "are meant to become, through community, nothing less than a single cosmic priest offering the universe to the Father." (*Is the Last Supper Finished?* p. 165.)

In the Christian Eucharist we are dealing with a great deal more than the proper arrangement of a church service, we are celebrating and expressing our friendship with God, into which we enter through the atonement accomplished by Jesus Christ. We are moving toward the final goal of man which our Lord, at the Last Supper, described by saying, "You will eat and drink at my table in my Kingdom" (Luke 22:30).

It is this relationship with God, at whose table we feast, which is the core of the eucharistic celebration. It is the

Lord's Supper, and we are his guests, called by him to the heavenly banquet. The purpose of the liturgical forms is to facilitate our participation in the sacred meal.

Meals, not only throughout history but in our own culture, take a variety of forms, from cook-outs to state banquets. All have been, or are being, used as models for the celebration of the Lord's Supper. Often in secular meals the human interchange, the social interpersonal relationships expressed at the table, are forced and artificial if not actually false. People are not free to say what they mean or to express their true feelings. They play the parts which society or the situation requires of them. Conversation is formal and stilted as the diners conceal themselves behind conventional masks.

When this is carried over to the sacred meal, not only social life but worship itself is destroyed. Before the God from whom no secrets are hid we cannot simply play a conventional part. Artificiality and conventionality are inconsistent with union and communion with Christ in his Church. This does not mean that forms and ceremonies ought to be abolished. Highly formal and ceremonial actions need be neither artificial nor empty of meaning. The kiss of the bride and groom at the wedding ceremony is both formal and ceremonial, but it is seldom an empty gesture. On the other hand, a studied "folksiness" and disregard for traditional patterns of behavior may be both. We can be as formal, as splendid, as simple, or as casual as we wish, as long as our actions really express what we intend, as long, that is, as we mean what we do.

"Style" in Worship Services

In a culture as variegated as ours is at present, not only will there be many differing ways in which people express their intentions naturally, there may well be no one style with which everyone can feel comfortable. What is normal and natural for a teenager will often be artificial and uncomfortable for his parents. The man in a tuxedo at the symphony may feel as comfortable as his neighbor who wears jeans and sits on the floor to listen to folk guitars. How can both participate fully and freely as fellow worshipers and communicants at the liturgy? Certainly neither must force the other to conform to his standards.

Many people will be happy with a variety of styles. Some will not. On some things we may simply agree to disagree. Most congregations today exhibit a variety of dress which would have been unthinkable a generation ago. There are things, nevertheless, on which we must agree or reach some working compromise if we are to worship together. The "style" of the service must be one in which many can participate.

A great many of the changes in the liturgy to which people react most violently are really changes in style and taste. Victorian music and art, for example, are not widely appreciated by contemporary Americans. Some hymns and some religious art, however, are so associated in our minds with the church of our childhood that we accept them without criticism, and we are quite resentful when someone who did not share our earlier experience, or who reacted rather differently to it, applies to them the standards of criticism which we ourselves accept in other areas. "Why don't we sing the old familiar hymns?" we ask, without asking whether the music is good or the words appropriate.

What we ask of the liturgy is that it serve as a vehicle of our approach to God in the Eucharist, rather than a roadblock. For Roman Catholics this goal was well ex-

Praying the Liturgy

pressed in the *Constitution on the Sacred Liturgy* (par. 50):

> The rite of the Mass is to be revised in such a way that the intrinsic nature and purpose of its several parts, as also the connection between them, can be more clearly manifested, and that devout and active participation of the faithful can be more easily accomplished.

Certainly this is what Christians of other churches also ask of their eucharistic rites: that they make plain the nature and purpose of what we do and promote devout and active participation. In the Liturgy of the Word, the good news of the gospel is proclaimed to those who hunger for the Word of Life, through the reading and preaching of the Holy Scripture. The liturgy spreads before the people the varied riches of the Word of God and provides a format in which they can hear, understand, and respond to them. In the Liturgy of the Sacrament we come as guests to the Lord's table, to celebrate his death and resurrection and to eat and drink his Body and Blood under the sacramental forms of Bread and Wine. We do this not simply as individuals but as his mystical Body, the Church, constituted by the presence of the Lord in our midst.

What liturgy best fulfills these goals? This is a question much easier to ask than to answer. It is certainly the object of the "new" liturgies to fulfill them. Their compilers have been at great pains to make their structure clear. Most liturgical commissions have followed the practical guidelines of the *Constitution on the Sacred Liturgy* (par. 50), either consciously or unconsciously:

> The rites are to be simplified, due care being taken to preserve their substance; elements which, with the passage of time, came to be duplicated, or were added with but little advantage, are now to be discarded; other elements which have suffered injury through accidents of history are now to be restored to the vigor which they had in the days of the holy Fathers, as may seem useful or necessary.

The traditional outline of the Eucharist given in Chapter I is the clear basis of most contemporary revisions of the liturgy. An opening hymn of praise, such as the Gloria in Excelsis, is followed by a prayer and the Scripture readings. Between the readings the congregation responds in psalm or hymn, and after them the homily provides a contemporary commentary and application. The Nicene Creed, when it is used, signifies the response of the Church to the Word of God in which the congregation identifies itself with the Catholic and Apostolic Church of the ages in the profession of a common gospel faith. Common prayer is then offered. It binds together those who profess a common faith, so that we may be more truly one when we make Eucharist. The Offertory, Consecration, Fraction, and Communion, as we have already seen, constitute the "doing this" in obedience to Christ's command and example. A post-Communion prayer of thanksgiving and a dismissal complete the rite.

As a matter of objective fact there can be little doubt that the new forms of service are clearer in their organization of material and more direct in their movement than the older forms. Their design is admirable and their purpose clear. Many people, nevertheless, do not feel "at home" in the new liturgies. They understand their theoretical excellence and appreciate the effort which has gone into their production, but, as one priest expressed it, "The old liturgy is where I live. I can relax and pray in it, because I am at home!" This attitude is in many ways natural. We are all products of the patterns of devotion in which we were brought up, and if we find them still congenial we do not wish to discard or change them.

Praying the Liturgy

I believe, however, that the introduction of new forms of worship can be a real occasion for spiritual growth. Different prayers, or different wordings of familiar prayers, bring to our attention aspects of the life of prayer which we have overlooked or neglected and give us a new insight into the meaning of our common action. The principal problem for many people, however, is not common but personal prayer. As a part of the medieval heritage of all Western Christians, we have tended not so much to pray the liturgy as to use the liturgy as the occasion for personal prayer. The preconciliar Roman Catholic with his rosary and the Episcopalian with his "book of devotion" were equally engaging in private prayer during the liturgy. Perhaps, more than anything else, we need to learn to pray the liturgy as common prayer.

The purpose of the opening hymn, or entrance song, is to help to gather the congregation, to direct our attention away from ourselves and our own thoughts to the assembly of the Church for its corporate worship. This is why a song is so effective at the beginning of the service. It literally calls us to participate. "Come let us sing to the Lord," proclaims the psalmist in one of the Church's earliest opening hymns, Psalm 95 (Venite Exultemus Domino). The opening prayer serves the same purpose, and it is by our participation in them that we become a part of the worshiping community and prepare ourselves for worship.

As we have seen in Chapter II, the reading of the Bible

is the core of the Liturgy of the Word, and prayerful listening is the best mode of participation. Ideally the entire church, including the bishop and his assisting clergy, listen to the Word of God as it is read by a reader, a lay person, from the Bible. It is unfortunately true that many readers do not read so that they can be understood, and that many churches have poor acoustics. It may be necessary for people to follow the words of the readings with their eyes, but this should always be to enhance listening, not to replace it.

Most churches seem to be afraid to allow the congregation time to reflect upon the Word of God in the lessons, and those in charge of planning services should remember that people need to assimilate what they have heard. There is no need to hurry into a vocal response, especially one which requires the participation of the entire congregation. *Services for Trial Use* mentions psalms as a first choice for use between the lessons, with hymns and anthems as alternatives. A responsorial psalm, sung by a solo voice, with the congregation repeating a refrain, or a psalm read responsively while the people remain seated, can be effective means of continuing the message of the readings. To pray during this portion of the liturgy means to listen to what is read and to think about its meaning.

A special word is in order about the Nicene Creed, which usually follows the sermon or homily on Sundays and festivals. This is the ecumenical statement of the Church's faith, adopted by the councils of the fourth century and recited by Christians to affirm their unity with that Church in the true faith. It is not intended to be an individual affirmation of faith, like the Apostles' Creed in Baptism, but the common expression of the faith of the Church. There is therefore an especial appropriateness in the increasing use of an ecumenically approved English text of that creed. It properly begins "We believe . . ." as all the prayers of the liturgy are in the plural. Even when we pray alone we say, "Our Father . . . give us this day our daily bread." The use of "We believe" follows the original text of the creed, as well as the ICET version. It had already been restored in the Episcopal Church in the 1967 Liturgy of the Lord's Supper, which prepared its own new translation of the creed, before the ICET text became available.

Private Prayer in the Liturgy

What place is there in the liturgy, then, for individual prayer? Some would say that there is none, but that goes too far. In the common prayers of the Church, the separate prayers of every individual are gathered up. The pauses provided in most prayers of intercession are intended to permit individuals to offer prayers for their own personal intentions, either silently, or aloud so that others may pray with them.

There are other places in the liturgy where silence provides an opportunity for private prayer. Before the general confession and at the breaking of the bread silence is particularly appropriate. In one case it provides us with an opportunity to think of our own sins, and in the other to reflect back on the Great Thanksgiving and to prepare for the reception of Communion. These prayers do not have to be in words. It is not necessary to recite a prayer, but to follow the suggestion of the psalmist, "Be still, then, and know that I am God" (Ps. 46:10). It is important that there be sufficient periods of silence during the liturgy. Often the directions of service books calling for times of silence are ignored. Revelation 8:1 says, "There was silence in heaven for about half an hour." Without attempting to solve the difficult questions which the book of Revelation raise, we may note that what is being described is an act of worship, and silence finds an important place in it. Silence not only provides us with an opportunity to speak to God, but with an opportunity to listen, so that we may hear his voice. Quakers and Pentecostals are not alone in believing that the Holy Spirit speaks to the Church assembled for prayer. It is part of the central tradition of Christian worship.

Roman Catholics have made effective use of silence following the distribution of Communion. A pause for silent prayer before the post-Communion hymn or prayer gives an opportunity for private prayer and recollection within the assembled group. Most congregations would benefit from this period of rest. A great deal has happened during the Eucharist, and we need time to "let it sink in." Many clergymen and organists seem to be afraid of silence, and feel that they must provide "background music" when no voice is reading prayers. Music can frequently be a real help to devotion, but listening to music is not silence.

Many churches have also revived the ancient practice of pausing between "Let us pray" and the beginning of the collect. This enables the people to accept the invitation to pray by doing so silently for a few moments, and restores the collect to its purpose of collecting and focusing the prayers of the congregation.

Ways of Praying the Liturgy

Prayer, like liturgy, is not a matter of words, although words play an important part in both. We pray in words, in wordless silence, and in our actions. Participating in the exchange of the peace, or in the offertory, or receiving

Communion are acts of prayer, whether or not we express them in words. Justin Martyr, in the passage quoted in Chapter I, speaks of the great "Amen" with which he and the rest of the congregation assented to the proclamation of the Great Thanksgiving by the president of the assembly. We too are called upon to say "Amen" to this prayer. This suggests strongly that the prayer of the congregation during the eucharistic prayer is active participation in the prayer the president prays in our name, joining in the acclamations in those prayers in which there are congregational responses, and in the Amen and the Lord's Prayer, with Justin's sense of making the words and prayer of the priest our own.

The reception of Communion is the supreme nonverbal prayer, in which we participate in the Eucharist of the Church and in the death and rising again of Christ. Whether we approach the altar in silence or with a glorious shout is largely a matter of taste and custom; it is the approaching which is itself the prayer.

Certainly a self-conscious wondering about what happens next is destructive of the spirit of prayer, but so is the empty repetition of familiar words. One of the faults of the images generated by the classic liturgies, such as the Book of Common Prayer or the Latin Mass, is that they are so strong in their royal imagery that we are apt to feel that worship is a court ceremonial, and that doing the wrong thing is disgraceful. We should come to our Father's house and feel comfortable and able to relax in his presence. This does not mean that splendor need be taken out of worship. No liturgy is more splendid than that of the Byzantine Church, and yet the easy familiarity with which the people participate is hard to find in even the most informal Western services.

Liturgical change is, of course, a nuisance. It upsets our established patterns of devotion, but perhaps those patterns need to be upset. Do we really pray the liturgy? Or do we pray at it? A liturgy which is more demanding of our participation is harder to ignore. If what we mean by prayer is saying our own personal prayers while the priest, the choir, and the acolytes celebrate the Eucharist, then indeed the old silent "low Mass," whether in English or in Latin, will give us more time to pray. But if we pray the liturgy, then the rite should help us by leading our minds and our bodies into common prayer. What kind of a liturgy can do this?

It must clearly be the liturgy of the Church throughout the ages (including the age in which we grew up), for a truly *new* liturgy, if we can pray it at all, will not make us a part of the prayer of the Church. It must also be the prayer of our own generation, one in which we can really mean what we say and do. In Chapter I we quoted the words of the anthropologist Margaret Mead:

> It has to be old, because otherwise it won't have had enough imagination expended on it. It has to be old to be available to everyone within that tradition. But it must be fresh enough so that it can contain new vision and fresh form.
>
> *The Ritual Expressions of the Cosmic Sense*, p. 11

This is precisely what the liturgy must be if we are to pray it—old and new. It cannot discard its past and still be the worship of the same Church. Neither can it fossilize so that it becomes a museum of a glorious past, not the living prayer of present and future generations. This means that it must be periodically revised and renewed. The process can be difficult to live through, but it is absolutely necessary if the liturgy is to remain alive.

Praying the Liturgy

Our goal in the process of liturgical change is to provide ourselves with as good a liturgy as we can, so that it may be the expression of our prayer. Future generations may well revise it again, but if we build firm on the solid foundations of an understanding of the meaning and purpose of worship, their revisions will be modernizations and adaptations to changed conditions, not major reconstructions.

One of the unfortunate side effects of "trial use" in the Episcopal Church has been the critical frame of mind it has instilled in worshipers. By looking critically at new forms of worship for the purpose of improving them, we sometimes find ourselves unable to pray. The liturgy is not to be gazed upon and admired or criticized, but to be prayed. It is common prayer. It gives us the words and actions by which we can pray together as the Body of Christ. We can, of course, do this with any liturgy. There has never been devised a form of public worship so poor that it made it impossible for *anyone* to pray, but obviously some forms make it easier than others. Words which we do not understand, or prayers which say things we do not wish to say, are substantial blocks to full participation in prayer. Familiar words, and prayers with long association with rites and occasions, give us an ease in praying. Unfamiliar ones, however excellent, may cause thought to stumble. On the other hand, familiar patterns can become monotonous and rote repetition replace inward prayer, while new turns of phrase may move us to new devotion.

There is no easy answer, and the liturgy cannot make men pray. All we can ask of it is that it make it as easy as possible, and not itself become an obstacle. But this principle is difficult, if not impossible, to apply in practice. Probably nothing in the "new" liturgies has caused as much adverse comment as the new ICET text of the "Our Father," yet some people have been brought to a new understanding of prayer, which had never meant much to them, by hearing and saying the words of the new version. It is a question for each individual and each congregation. "How can we most effectively pray the liturgy?" And it is a task for each parish to put that answer to work in its own worship.

VI
Go Forth into the World

It is sometimes suggested to those involved in the process of revising liturgical forms that this is an activity comparable to the rearrangement of the deck chairs on a sinking ship. The Church, they are sure, is in its last hours, and revising a liturgy which is used by ever diminishing numbers of people is wasted effort.

Certainly there are enthusiasts who speak of liturgical reform as if it would solve the problems of the Church, and probably those of the world as well. Their claims should be much more modest if they wish them to be taken seriously. The late Arthur C. Lichtenberger, then Presiding Bishop of the Episcopal Church, included this paraphrase of the prophet Amos in his address to the liturgical conference held in Madison, Wisconsin, in 1958:

> I hate, I despise your parish communions and I will take no delight in your public baptisms. Yea, though ye offer me bread and wine I will not accept them: neither will I regard the corporate recitation of the Prayer of Humble Access. . . . But let justice roll down like waters and righteousness like an overflowing stream.
>
> Massey H. Shepherd, (ed.),
> *The Liturgical Renewal of the Church,* p. 119

Church Renewal

The real concern of the twentieth-century Liturgical Movement is not with the reform of the liturgy, but with the renewal of the Church. The conviction that worship is central to the life and mission of the Church produces the concern with the reform and renewal (not simply the revision) of the liturgy.

> The Liturgical Movement is grounded on this very principle: the worship of God precedes man's witness in the world.... It is only after we have raised our hearts and minds to God in complete adoration that we receive the power and (as we say nowadays) the "know-how" to work for the spread of God's Kingdom on earth.
>
> Frank S. Cellier, *Liturgy Is Mission*, p. 16

This is, of course, the pattern both of the "Our Father" and of the Summary of the Law. In the Lord's Prayer we hallow God's name, and then move on to praying for the Kingdom, while the Summary of the Law moves from love of God as the *first* commandment to love of neighbor as the *second*. It is of course true that worship has not always borne fruit in action, just as it is true that the expression of the love of God has not always led to love of neighbor. I John 4:20 warns us, "If someone says, 'I love God,' but hates his brother, he is a liar." Worship which remains locked within the church building is equally perverse.

Christian Worship and Christian Living

It is when the Church makes Eucharist that it is most itself. This is its characteristic and representative action in which it manifests itself as one with Christ, the Head of the Church, in his eternal action as the Apostle and High Priest of our faith (cf. Heb. 3:1). But the celebration of the liturgy does not exhaust the activity of the Church. Christian worship must be both the fruit and the source of Christian living. The unity in Christ signified at the altar must be expressed in action and lifestyle, and that expression in turn makes it possible for us to celebrate the Eucharist as "one family in Christ." We do not engage in common prayer as isolated individuals, but as members one of another in the Body of Christ. This is what Bishop Lichtenberger was saying in the address already quoted (*op. cit.,* p. 119):

> When we are unaware of the social implications of the liturgy, or ignore these implications, we fail to that extent to offer ourselves to God as "a reasonable, holy and living sacrifice." For each time we receive the Body and Blood of our Lord, we are by that act sent to be witnesses to Him before the world. This does not mean that we are to lead pious lives but that we are to be in the thick of the struggle for justice and freedom and peace.

Traditionally, liturgies have ended with a dismissal, sending the people out into the world to "show forth thy praise not only with our lips but in our lives." The name most commonly used by the majority of Christians for the Eucharist, the Mass, is derived from the Latin *missa,* which means *sent.* It is part of the dismissal of the Latin Mass, "Ite, missa est," which sends the people of God forth from the altar into the world. It is related to the *mission* of the Church and to its apostolic commission: "As the Father sent me, so I send you" (John 20:21). The Greek word for *send* is *apostello,* and an apostle is one who is sent. The dismissal sends the assembled Church out to its mission, to its apostolate, to be the Body of Christ in the world.

This does not mean that we are to spend the rest of the week trying to act as if we were still in church, but rather, to remember that we come together to worship, not as individuals but as people already enmeshed in a web of society, and it is the entire context of our daily lives which is offered to the Father to be sanctified through Jesus Christ, in the Holy Spirit, so that we may in truth live as Christians in the world.

The French Oratorian Louis Bouyer, in a book which was most appropriately called in its English edition *Life and Liturgy*, wrote:

> Perhaps the greatest, and certainly the most difficult problem for liturgical piety is the one which awaits us when we go out of the church after the liturgical celebration is finished. For, if there is one point our study has brought out, it is that the importance of the liturgical celebration itself implies a correlative importance in what we do, after the liturgical celebration, in daily living. The Mystery that is always present and always active in the liturgy can only show its presence and manifest its activity through the whole life of Christians, through that Cross and that resurrection which are their permanent "witness" to the world.
>
> *Liturgical Piety*, p. 257 (American edition)

Fr. A. Gabriel Hebert, S.S.M., who first brought the contemporary Liturgical Movement to the popular consciousness of the Church of England, wrote in 1935:

> The Christian liturgy . . . is a kind of meeting-point, in which all the elements of the Church are seen in their right perspective. . . . Our business is therefore to disen-

tangle so far as we may the essential principles of the Church's worship and life, and to see these in relation to the actual life of men and the order of human society. We have not only to consider what we do with Christ in the Church, but what He wills to do with us in the street. The Church has indeed the key to the street. Too often she seems inclined to use it to lock herself in.

Liturgy and Society, p. 182

Bishop Lichtenberger, commenting on this passage, suggested that the Episcopal Church has not only buried its talent, but often devoted its attention to embroidering the napkin in which it has done so.

Action Follows Worship

In point of fact, these words have not gone unheeded. The 1960s were a time of immensely renewed social action both on the part of the institutional Church and of individual Christians acting as members of the Body of Christ, and the need of the present is not so much to defend social action as it is to remind social activists that action *follows* worship. It is true that liturgical renewal cannot by itself renew the Church, but if the worship of the Christian people is dead, then the heart has been cut out of their religion. It is when liturgy and life are most one in both inner reality and outward effects that the Church is most alive.

We need to look again at the terms of our Commission:

> "You are witnesses of these things. And I myself will send upon you what my Father has promised. But you must wait in the city until the power from above comes down upon you. . . ." They worshiped him and went

back into Jerusalem, filled with great joy, and spent all
their time in the Temple giving thanks to God.

Luke 24:48–49, 52–53

It is this power of God, Christ's gift to his Church, which we need before we can go forth. In the words of a contemporary eucharistic prayer:

Let the grace of this Holy Communion
make us one body, one spirit in Christ,
that we may worthily serve the world in his name.

Authorized Services 1973, p. 79

This is not a prayer which finds a place in most traditional liturgies. It has, in fact, been criticized as representing a passing concern of the mid-twentieth-century. I do not believe that is true. As we have seen in Chapter II, the scope of Christian worship is intended to be cosmic. Through Christ we can do what man on his own failed to do. We can offer the world to God. The Incarnation of the Son of God has as its goal the salvation not of the Church, but of the world (cf. John 3:16). We are called to a share in his priesthood, his apostolate, his mission to the world. This was very evident to the early Christians, who did in fact set forth to convert the world—with unbelievable success. The second- or third-century Letter to Diognetus expresses this consciousness of mission straightforwardly:

To put it simply: What the soul is in the body, that Christians are in the world. . . . The soul dwells in the body but does not belong to the body, and Christians dwell in the world but do not belong to the world. . . . The soul is shut up in the body, and yet itself holds the body together; while Christians are restrained in the world as in a prison, and yet themselves hold the world together. . . . It is to no less a post than this that God has ordered them, and they must not try to evade it.

Diognetus 6, *Early Christian Fathers*,

Changing Views of Christianity

It was with the coming of what we call Christendom and the established Church that this world mission seemed to grow dim in Christian thought. From the time of the conversion of Constantine until the present century, Christian mission has meant sending someone else "over there" to convert "them," or even going oneself. It has been assumed that only the lands on the fringes of civilization—northern Europe and Britain in the Middle Ages, the Orient, Africa, and the South Seas in more modern times—were in need of evangelization. Europe, and later North America, were presumed to be Christian. The secular state to the present day accepts a baptismal certificate as proof of native-born citizenship. Medieval Europe saw itself as a Christian commonwealth of which church and state were simply two aspects. Sixteenth-century England saw itself in the same way, and there can be little doubt that Henry VIII saw himself as both pope and emperor of his most Christian kingdom. To be a citizen was to be a church member.

These are the terms in which the classical liturgies, Roman, Anglican, Orthodox, Lutheran, and Reformed, speak. Today "Christendom" no longer exists. The words of the Prayer Book Catechism speak of a world in which we no longer live:

> My duty towards my Neighbor is... To submit myself to
> all my governors, teachers, spiritual pastors and masters:
> To order myself lowly and reverently to all my betters.
> ... And to do my duty in that state of life unto which it
> shall please God to call me.
>
> Book of Common Prayer, pp. 579f.

This, of course, is not the whole of the Catechism's teaching about love of neighbor, but it reflects a spirit foreign to contemporary thought. It suggests that the status quo is itself just, right, and according to God's plan. It suggests strongly that we should pull on our own oar and not rock the boat, certainly not by inquiring why we are chosen to row while others give orders or ride as passengers.

The nineteenth century began to challenge this view of Christianity, and Christian Social Action became a part of church life about the turn of the century. The social concern expressed in the encyclicals of Leo XIII is matched by the formation of such organizations as the Church Association for the Advancement of the Interests of Labor in the Episcopal Church and by the rise of the Social Gospel in American Protestantism.

It may be overstating the case to suggest that it was the loss of the social dimension of the liturgy which made possible the perversion of the Christian gospel by a lack of concern for the social order over so many centuries, but it is precisely the entire social dimension of worship which was lost in the later Middle Ages, and often not recovered at the Reformation. The Abbé Michenneau, one of the prophets of the French church in the days following World War II who saw their own country as a primary missionary area, described a typical low Mass in Paris in 1949 this way:

Go Forth into the World

> A few men are standing up at the back of the church and looking around. Further up, the church is pretty well filled, with women mostly; some are saying their beads. . . . Some are reading prayer books or missals. Some are seated while the rest kneel; for no apparent reason there are periodic reverses of position. . . . Obviously the people in that church are not a community, but a mere collection of isolated individuals, praying individually as best they can.
>
> *Revolution in a City Parish*, p. 26

I think it fair to say that in the United States there was more concern for uniformity of posture, but the isolation of worshipers was just as real. Children were taught to ignore their fellow worshipers, to follow the service in their Prayer Book, to say their own prayers and, above all, not to disturb anyone else. If there was communication between priest and people, there was none between members of the congregation. The Calvinist believed just as firmly that it was the duty of the minister to pray for the people as the Catholic did that it was the duty of the priest to say Mass for them. The sense of the Church as the community of the faithful assembled for worship and sent forth to work and serve was scarcely evident. Where a liturgical dismissal remained, it was not seen as sending the people forth, but as letting them go until the next hour of prayer. Its function had been so obscured that it was missing altogether from the liturgy of the Book of Common Prayer, while in the Latin Mass it had ceased to be the final act of the service. Although the words were spoken for those who could understand the Latin, they were followed by a blessing, a reading from the Gospel, and several prayers, at the very least.

The Post-Christian World

Today there is general recognition that we live in a post-Christian world. We cannot expect the state to proclaim the gospel for us, or even serve as "defender of the Faith." If Christian standards are to be the standards of the world, it can only be because Christians make them so. This does not mean that the Church as an institution must take a stand on every contemporary issue. Often this may be both impossible and highly undesirable. It does mean that those Christians who assemble for Sunday Eucharist and are sent forth to be the Church in the world have an obligation to take a stand, to be, in Bishop Lichtenberger's words, "in the thick of the struggle for justice and freedom and peace." This is a task, not of the hierarchy but of the baptized Christian living in the world.

The classic liturgies give us a picture of a hierarchically ordered Church, but they never suppose that the hierarchy is the Church. The ministry is set *within* the Church, not over it. The liturgy is the action of all the people of God, in which everyone has his place, not something performed by the clergy for the laity. Baptism, not ordination, makes us churchmen. Witness is not the exclusive mark of any order within the Church. Catechumens not yet baptized have borne their witness as well as popes and bishops. St. James reminds us:

> Suppose there are brothers or sisters who need clothes and don't have enough to eat. What good is there in saying to them, "God bless you! Keep warm and eat well!"—if you don't give them the necessities of life?
>
> James 2:15–16

Our goal is the redemption of the world. This involves us in more than preaching, and pious living. Feeding the hungry can never replace preaching the Gospel, but it may well be the precondition of its being heard. Just as all of life is properly brought to the liturgy to be offered to God, so from it flows all of life, as by the power of Christ's dying and rising again we seek to transform the world.

All of this seems to have come a long way from liturgical change, and yet, when the *Constitution on the Sacred Liturgy* set out in its opening paragraph to give reasons for the sweeping change of the Roman Catholic liturgy which it inaugurated, it gave these four:

1. to intensify daily growth in Christian living
2. to respond to the needs of the present
3. to contribute to the unity of all Christian Churches
4. to strengthen the missionary outreach of the Church toward all men.

Certainly these are equally the concerns of all Christians, regardless of ecclesiastical label. The fathers of Vatican Council II believed, not without reason, that the place to begin this program of church renewal was with the reform of the liturgy. The Church today is trying to seek out the world and to speak to it, with relevance and cogency, the living and life-giving Word of the gospel of Jesus Christ, by whose power it can and will be saved. That Word is proclaimed and made present primarily in the celebration of the liturgy. It is so that liturgy may best speak to men in this changing world of the unchanging and unchangeable God that its reform and renewal are so important.

None of us today can properly evaluate the changes

presently being made in our forms of worship. Our perspective is too short. Fortunately, our mistakes can be corrected. The liturgy is not unchangeable. Its regular renewal and reform is an important missionary activity of the priestly people of God, and the decision not to change inherited forms is as much an act of renewal as the decision to change them. The Dismissal in the "trial liturgy" of the Episcopal Church has three alternatives. All express aspects of our task:

> Go forth into the world,
> rejoicing in the power of the Spirit.
>
> Go in peace to love and serve the Lord.
>
> Let us go forth in the Name of Christ.

We, clergy as well as laity, are sent into the world to love and serve the Lord, but it is only in the name of Christ and in the power of the Spirit that we can do so. We receive this power, not by attending a church service, whether in the "new" or the "old" form, but by offering our lives, individually and corporately, in penitence, praise, and thanksgiving, in union with the perfect sacrifice of Christ once offered, and in communion with him and one another. From this Eucharist the Risen Lord sends us forth in the power of the Holy Spirit to serve him joyfully in his world, the world which he himself offers to the Father in the eternal cosmic Eucharist. It is this which the liturgy celebrates and seeks to proclaim, and the better accomplishing of this is the goal of all liturgical change.

Leader's Guide for group use of *Liturgical Change: How Much Do We Need?*

Purpose of the Course

- To help participants come to terms with liturgical change and its meaning for them
- To help participants identify criteria for evaluating worship and to apply those criteria to their own liturgical experiences
- To help participants acquire some skills in worship, so that they are better able to pray the liturgy

Leadership

As leader, your task in these sessions is to help group members understand what they have read and clarify their own ideas. You do not have to defend any particular liturgical practice, theory, or style, but you should try to be fair to both the liturgies you discuss and the group members who may disagree with you and each other. The session outlines are purely suggestive. Be prepared to move with the group and help them deal with the material in their own way. On the other hand, these sessions are designed to help the group deal positively with the material and provide channels for constructive criticism, so that the sessions do not degenerate into "gripe sessions" about the new liturgies, or the manner in which the parish celebrates them.

Time, Place, and Setting

The sessions are planned for a forty-five-minute period. If a longer period is used, the time frame might be slightly expanded. It is *not* recommended that the sessions be combined into three sessions of an hour and a half, however. The sessions may be held on a Sunday morning, or as part of an evening study program. It is highly desirable that they follow a service of worship, either the regular Sunday Eucharist, or a special service held for the group. If it is not possible to celebrate the liturgy before each of the sessions, it should at least be part of the first and last sessions. The sessions are designed for a small group. Ten to twelve participants is ideal. If the group reaches more than twice that size, it should be divided into smaller groups.

The room in which the sessions are to be held should be arranged to encourage discussion. Chairs are best placed in a circle, or around a large table. Any suggestion in the arrangement of the furniture that the leader will be lecturing to a class should be carefully avoided.

Useful Resources

The leader and each participant will need a copy of this book, or at least have access to a copy between sessions.

For cassette-users this book is also available in a three-cassette recording from Catacomb Cassettees (15 16th St., N.E., Atlanta, Georgia 30309). Several copies of the "new" and "old" liturgies should be available for reference during the sessions. For Episcopalians this means *Authorized Services 1973, Services for Trial Use,* and the Book of Common Prayer should be provided. For Roman Catholics the new *Ordo Missae* in any convenient form and the Tridentine Mass as found in the old Latin-English missals would be helpful. For Lutherans *The Service Book and Hymnal* (or *The Lutheran Hymnal*) and the Contemporary Worship pamphlets of the Inter-Lutheran Commission on Worship would be appropriate. Those who use other liturgies than these should choose the appropriate books. In all cases a copy of *Authorized Services 1973, Services for Trial Use,* and *Prayers, Thanksgivings, and Litanies* (Prayer Book Studies 25) would be useful for reference. All are available from Church Hymnal Corporation, 800 Second Avenue, New York, New York 10017.

It is helpful if at least one copy of each book listed in Books for Further Reading (p. 118) is available to the group. The leader will probably wish to consult them in his preparation, and participants may be interested in "going deeper" into some point after the session.

A blackboard or newsprint will be needed for each session. Paper and pencils will be needed for some sessions. Name tags should be provided at the first session, and thereafter as needed.

Session I: Change and the Unchangeable

PURPOSE OF THIS SESSION

To help the participants to express clearly their feelings about changes being made in the liturgy.

Procedure

This session is most easily held following a celebration of a "new liturgy," either at the regular Sunday Eucharist or at a special midweek service arranged for the group.

In most Episcopal parishes this would mean the "Second Service" Eucharist, but it should be whatever service exemplifies the liturgical change with which the group is concerned. This will give them a specific example of liturgical change to examine together, and on which to focus their discussion.

This is an introductory session, so introductions are important. Unless the group already know each other well, name tags should be provided. They may be even more important if the group are slightly acquainted with each other than if they are complete strangers, since they may be embarrassed to ask each other's names. Each group member (including the leader) is given a tag when he arrives.

Begin the session by introducing yourself (even if you assume that you are already known to the group), explaining the time schedule, the dates and places of the sessions, and other necessary information. Pass out copies of the course and go through it with the group (or if you prefer, wait and do this at the end of the session).

Ask each member of the group to choose another member to work with during this session. (If members of the same family are in the group, they should be discouraged from choosing each other.)

Each pair devotes five minutes to interviewing one another. The interview should include the other person's name, and such other personal information as seems appropriate, but its purpose is to ask the other person, "How do you feel about the new liturgy?" The pairs do not discuss the subject with each other, but simply find out how the other feels.

At the end of five minutes, each person in turn introduces the one he interviewed to the group, and states as simply as possible the other person's feelings about the liturgy.

As leader, do not evaluate what is said. Do not attempt to answer any questions asked, but simply allow the participants to report one another's views. Check with the interviewees to be sure that they are satisfied with the presentation of their views.

Then ask the group to react to two statements you will read:

> 1. There was never anything by the wit of man so well devised, or so well established, which (in continuance of time) hath not been corrupted: as (among other things) it may plainly appear by the common prayers of the Church, commonly called divine service.
>
> Book of Common Prayer, 1549
>
> 2. The liturgy is made up of immutable elements divinely instituted, and of elements subject to change. These not only may but ought to be changed with the passage of time if they have suffered from the intrusion of anything out of harmony with the inner nature of the liturgy, or have become unsuited to it.
>
> *Constitution on the Sacred Liturgy,* 1963

If these quotations elicit spontaneous reactions, encourage them. After a while, ask the participants to list some of the changes they notice in the liturgy.

Record changes mentioned on the newsprint or blackboard, in a single column down the left side. On the rest of the board make three columns: positive (+), negative (−), and don't know (0). Ask the participants to vote on each of the listed changes. Where there is wide divergence of opinion, ask the group members to explain to the others what their votes mean.

If some change is predominently voted 0, it may be appropriate to try to find out if the votes mean "don't know" or "don't care."

Every opportunity must be given to the participants to express their feelings and to explain their divergent views to one another within the limits of the available time. You may answer direct questions of fact ("what" questions), but should avoid answering "why" questions, or evaluating the reactions of the participants. Resist the temptation to "instruct" the group in the meaning of liturgical changes. You will probably be saved from this mistake by lack of time.

At the end of the session, remind the participants to read the first chapter of the background reading. If you have not already distributed the copies of the course, do so now, pointing out the chapter to be read before the next session.

SESSION II: What Do We Want to Do in Our Worship?

In the first session participants were encouraged to express their feelings about changes in the liturgy. This time try to move beyond "I like this" or "I don't like that." See if you can articulate more objective standards for judging worship.

PURPOSE OF THIS SESSION

To identify some criteria for evaluating worship and try to apply these criteria to familiar services.

PROCEDURE

Begin the session by reviewing with the participants the discussion of criteria for worship in the background reading. "Criteria are the standards by which we evaluate anything, by which we judge whether it is good or bad. It is important for us to identify the standards we use in evaluating services of worship in order to carry our discussion beyond the expression of likes and dislikes. Last time we identified changes in the liturgy and expressed our reactions to them. Today we shall try to go one step farther."

Be prepared, or ask a group member to be prepared, to record the results of a brain-storming session on criteria for worship. Write down the suggested criteria on newsprint or the blackboard. The list as in Session I should be a single column to the left, so that space remains to make marks after the items.

Ask the group to suggest criteria for evaluating liturgies: By what standards do you evaluate a service of worship?

In the first part of the session contributions should not be discussed, but simply listed on the newsprint (or a blackboard), as many as possible. If suggestions come slowly, remind them of those suggested on pp. 19–20 of the background reading. You may read the short passage from the *Constitution on the Sacred Liturgy*. The group need not accept any of the criteria suggested in the background reading. In rejecting them, they will come up with others.

Not over five minutes should be spent in listing criteria. Once the list is obtained, ask the group to discuss the criteria. A procedure similar to that used in the first session can be employed.

Ask participants whether they consider each suggested standard important (mark in the + column), unimportant or indifferent (make a mark in the 0 column), or if they reject it as a standard (−). It is possible that some of the criteria may contradict others. One may feel flexibility and variety are important, while another considers uniformity essential.

There may be group consensus on some points. On others there may be violent disagreement. It is not important that the group members be of one mind, but it is important that they understand what each is saying. Urge group members to explain the meaning and importance of their criteria to the rest of the group. This is especially necessary when criteria are warmly supported by some and totally rejected by others.

Approximately twenty minutes may be devoted to this part of the exercise. The remainder of the session is devoted to an examination of the liturgy with which the participants are familiar in the light of their criteria. Decide in advance what liturgy will be most helpful to discuss. In most cases it will be the normal Sunday morning liturgy of the parish. Copies of the liturgy should be provided for reference.

Ask group members to apply their criteria to the liturgy. In what way does it meet their standards? In what way does it fail to meet them? Probably there will be some criteria which cannot be applied to the liturgy in so general a way. If quality preaching is a criterion, for example, only a discussion of specific sermons could apply it, and this would not serve the purpose of the session. The leader may have to steer the discussion away from criticism of specific preachers, readers, or musicians. This can be done by asking the members to use specifics to illustrate the criteria. For instance, "Sermons should illuminate the gospel" might be someone's criteria for a good sermon.

If the session bogs down in a discussion of the words of the new liturgies, or new *vs.* old words, remind the group that words will be the topic of the next two sessions, and that they can deal more profitably with other aspects of worship in this session.

Leader's Guide

Suggest to the participants that they look for strengths and weaknesses in the service, in the light of the criteria they have listed. It is unlikely that the group will have time to complete their evaluation of the liturgy in the light of their criteria. Remember, your goal is not to revise the liturgy this week, but to help the participants identify the criteria by which they evaluate their own worship. Applying them to specific worship experiences is not the work of a session, but of a lifetime.

Before the end of the session, ask the participants to look again at their criteria in the light of their discussion, and see if they wish to revise their views, add new criteria, or alter those previously accepted. The session closes with the assignment of Chapter II of the background reading.

SESSION III: What Do We Want to Say in Our Common Prayers?

In the last session the group was asked to try to identify criteria for "good" worship, and to begin to apply those criteria to a particular liturgical experience. The group should be ready to look more closely at the content of our prayers—*what* it is we pray about.

PURPOSE OF THIS SESSION

To discover what we and our fellow worshipers need to pray for today, in order to see how well our current liturgies help us pray.

PROCEDURE

Flexibility of structure is essential in this session. The participants must feel free to ask their own questions and deal with their own concerns, rather than feeling they must deal with a fixed agenda. It is more important that they deal with the material at their own pace than that they examine all of the prayers suggested.

In the background reading a number of basic questions are raised about the common prayers of the Church:
- How much flexibility do we want in our common prayers?
- How much flexibility can we handle?
- Do our prayers say what we wish to say in the way we wish to say it?
- Do we wish to add new petitions not in our present forms?

A number of specific questions are also raised, such as:
- Should we not pray for non-Christian as well as Christian rulers?
- How much freedom should the individual priest, or congregation, have to alter the Eucharistic Prayer?

These may inspire group members to raise other related questions. Encourage them to discuss their ideas freely with one another. You can encourage depth of exchange by asking such questions as:
- What does this mean to you?
- How do you feel about that?

One way to start is to read the statement of basic topics for intercession from *Services for Trial Use,* and to ask the group to criticize and expand it with specific suggestions of objects for prayer:

Prayer is offered with intercession for:
 The Universal Church and all its members
 The Nation and all in authority
 The welfare of the world
 The concerns of the local community
 Those who suffer and those in trouble
 The departed (with commemoration of a saint when appropriate)

Cf. *Services for Trial Use,* pp. 70, 93, 307; *Authorized Services 1973,* pp. 62, 83, 182

Ask a recorder to list in one column on newsprint or a blackboard those items considered by the group to be important. In a second column he or she should list those the group wishes included occasionally, and (if appropriate) list in a third column any they feel should be left out.

Specific texts of prayers of intercession can then be examined. The Prayer for the Whole State of Christ's Church and a contemporary litany of intercession would be appropriate models to look at, or other forms familiar to the group can be used. Have copies of the texts ready for the group to use.

As the discussion continues, the recorder can make additions or corrections to the list of what we want to pray for.

Questions to be asked about the prayer texts include:
- What does this suggest to you?
- Do we wish to say it?
- Are there other things we wish to pray for instead, or in addition?

If they do not arise spontaneously from the examination of the forms, you may ask questions like:
- How specific should we be in our prayers?
- What do you think about having members of the congregation mention the names of their friends?
- How do you feel about praying about items in the morning newspaper?
- Should we always use the same form of prayer, or should we make use of alternatives?

You may have time to examine the Eucharistic Prayer, but don't push the group to do this if it wishes to devote all of its time to the prayers of intercession. The outline of the Eucharistic Prayer given in Chapter II, pp. 36–37, will focus attention on its various elements. The same questions used in examining the intercession may be asked again.

The list of "what we want to say in our common prayers" will be used for the next session. Save the newsprint, or if it is written on a blackboard it should be copied and saved.

Take note of subjects of prayer important to the group which are not in the existing forms. Also note subjects which are not considered appropriate for use by Christians today. These notes may be communicated to the parish or diocesan liturgical commission. In the Episcopal Church specific suggestions from study groups for improving forms of prayer are always welcomed by the Standing Liturgical Commission, and should be sent through the diocesan liturgical commission. Specific, well-thought-out suggestions from members of the congregation are welcomed by those charged with preparing liturgies.

At the close of the session, tell the group that the next session will be about "how" we say what we want to say in our prayers. Ask them to bear in mind the subjects they have indicated they want prayed for, while they read Chapter III. At the next session we shall try to put our prayers into words.

SESSION IV: The Problem of Words

Last session the group looked at the "what" of prayer. Now we are ready to consider questions of style, the "how" of prayer.

Leader's Guide

PURPOSE OF THIS SESSION

To practice putting our prayers into words, in order to gain some understanding of the problems facing those who are writing new liturgies.

PROCEDURE

The section in Daniel B. Stevick's *Language in Worship* entitled "The Church's Prayers and the Human Condition" (pp. 75–81) will be helpful background reading for the leader of this session. Duplicate the following part of that passage and distribute it to the members of the group at the beginning of the session (a member of the group can read it aloud):

> History has rendered the terms in which [the Prayer for the Whole State of Christ's Church] prays for Church and society unusable. . . . They are sixteenth-century terms with the order of the petitions reflecting the social order of medieval Christendom then on the point of passing away: Christendom, kings and those appointed by them, bishops and those appointed by them, and finally the lay people who are no more responsible for the direction of the Church than they are for the direction of the State. These terms describe a static authoritarian society; they do not engage us with our more dynamic, participatory society for which we intend to pray. . . .
>
> No one can justly complain if a liturgy drawn up in the preindustrial, prescientific sixteenth century did not see the problems or define the human good in ways that suit our contemporary situation exactly. Indeed, we can be grateful that, despite its identification with a specific past moment, the prayer has held up as well as it has. But when modern revisions fail to describe the

> modern world for which they are written, complaints can well be lodged. . . .
>
> The world we express in our intercessions should not be a different world from the one we live in at other times. . . . A prayer which takes account largely of the concerns of the wise, the powerful, the well-born, and the things that are must ask whether it is a prayer for Christ's catholic church.

Then ask the group to divide into subgroups of five or six. If there are less than ten members in the group, they remain as a single group, but ten should divide into two groups of five, twelve into two groups of six, fifteen into three groups of five, etc.

Ask the subgroups to examine the Prayer for the Whole State of Christ's Church in the light of Stevick's statement, the background reading of Chapter III, their own list of topics for prayer prepared in the previous session, and any other data they wish to bring to bear on it.

The question is: "What image of our society do we obtain from this prayer?" This might be restated as, "What kind of world does this prayer pray for? Is it the world in which *we* really live?"

After five minutes of discussion, direct their attention to some particular contemporary prayer of intercession, such as Intercessions I or V in *Services for Trial Use* or *Authorized Services*, and ask them to look at it in the light of the same questions they have asked about the Prayer for the Church.

Five to eight additional minutes should be allotted for this discussion. Give a warning two minutes before the end of the discussion period, so they can bring their discussion to a close. Ask each group to report briefly to the total group, on their discussion. Stevick's critique of the intercession of *The Liturgy of the Lord's Supper* should

Leader's Guide

help you respond to the reports of the subgroups.

It is not necessary that the subgroups come to consensus, nor that any clear answers to the questions emerge, but only that they be thoughtfully considered. Withhold comments of your own until the groups have reported. If the group is too small to break into subgroups, the leader should ask them to try and summarize their discussion, and then help them to reflect upon it.

Then direct the group's attention to the lists of topics for prayer they made in Session III. In the light of their background reading of Chapter III and their discussion in the subgroups, ask each person to try to write a short prayer dealing with one or more of the subjects on the group list.

First, ask each person to choose a topic for prayer from the list made last session.

Second, review with the group the collect form of prayer. It may be helpful to explain the collect structure simply in this way:

1. We begin with an address to God: "O God . . . ," "Almighty Father . . .," or in some such way.

2. We add a clause describing God. In traditional language prayers it begins, "who. . . ." More contemporary forms often make it a separate sentence. It says something about God which is related to the main petition of the prayer, or gives the occasion for offering prayer.

3. Then comes the petition. This is the main core of the prayer, what we are asking for. It often begins, "Grant . . ." or "Give us, we pray. . . ."

4. This is often followed by a purpose clause giving the reason for the request: "in order that . . ." or "that we may. . . ."

5. The collect closes with a doxology, usually, "through Jesus Christ our Lord, who lives and reigns with you and the Holy Spirit, one God, now and forever."

In writing a prayer it is easiest to begin with the petition (3) and purpose clause (4), then to go back and decide how best to address God, and finally to add the doxology.

You may wish to read to the group the two versions of the Christmas collect at the beginning of Chapter III as examples of two prayer styles, or you may have others at hand which relate more directly to the specific concerns of the group. Each member should compose his or her own prayer in the style he or she prefers.

About fifteen minutes should be allowed for the group to write their prayers. Those who wish to do so may be asked to read their prayers to the group in the final minutes of the session. No one should be compelled to read his prayer. The object is not to embarrass the participants, but to help them to understand what goes into the writing of public prayers. *Do not criticize individual prayers.*

If there is time, suggest that the group compose a corporate prayer. This can be encouraged, but don't force it.

If the group members felt unable to finish their prayers in the time available, encourage them to take them home and complete them. If they did finish, suggest they try again, either with the same or another topic. If the first attempt was in "traditional" style, the second might be in "contemporary," or vice versa. Time will be allowed at the beginning of Session V for the reading of these prayers.

The leader concludes the session by asking everyone to read Chapter IV of the background reading, and by encouraging them to work on a prayer they might be willing to read at the beginning of the next session. (Make sure no one leaves with the impression he will be *required* to read his prayer next time, or you may lose some group members.)

Leader's Guide

SESSION V: Unity and Uniformity

Last session's exercise in prayer writing probably revealed that even in a relatively small group, there is a wide diversity in the way people express themselves in prayer. That experience should prepare the group to face the question of unity and uniformity.

PURPOSE OF THIS SESSION

To explore the question of how much diversity is necessary and possible, and how much conformity should be required in the liturgical practice of the Church.

PROCEDURE

The leader begins the session by asking those who have composed prayers to read them to the group, if they are willing. If no one is willing to read his own prayer, the leader may try to compose a prayer with the group. (Review the simple directions in Session IV.)

Ask the group about the ease or difficulty they found in writing prayers. Then introduce the question of "traditional" and "contemporary" styles. Do group members see value in both styles? This question may serve as a bridge to the larger question of uniformtity.

If some in the group prefer one prayer style and some another, ask if they can see both styles co-existing in the same church? the same parish? the same service? If the entire group should consider the same style to be preferable, you may suggest some of the advantages of the other style, or raise the possibility of using both.

Ultimately, the question to be discussed is: How much uniformity is needed for the unity of the Church, and how much flexibility is needed and can be managed? By this time your group will have developed a character of their own and you will probably have a "feel" for how to get them to discuss this subject most fruitfully.

You might ask a series of questions which call for definite conclusions, such as:

- Should we adopt a new liturgy and impose it, so that it is uniformly used throughout the Church? or should we continue a large number of options?

This general question can be made more specific by asking questions of this sort:

- Should there be a single eucharistic liturgy which everyone in the Church is to use without deviation? If it is desirable, is it practicable?
- Should contemporary and traditional language services (such as the First and Second Services of *Services for Trial Use*) be available as complete alternatives? If not, which one should be abandoned?
- Should the people's responses during the liturgy always be the same (e.g., "And also with you." "It is right to give him thanks and praise.")?
- Should there be alternative prayers of intercession? Must they all be from "the book" or may priests and/or congregations compose their own?
- What are the pros and cons of alternative eucharistic prayers? Should the use of prayers not in "the book" be permitted on special occasions?
- Is there any place for specially composed prayers in the corporate worship of the Church?

Encourage the participants to explain why they feel as they do, and to listen to the explanations of others. The purpose of the discussion is not so much to have the group agree upon answers as it is to help them to see the variety of possible answers, and the reasons for them. You may want to express opinions not otherwise represented, or simply help group members articulate their opinions.

Leader's Guide

No conclusions should be drawn, but the questions allowed to remain as open as the group will permit.

Conclude the session by asking the participants to read Chapter V of the background reading.

SESSION VI: Praying the Liturgy

In these sessions we have been led to take a critical, thoughtful look at liturgy. This time we want to turn our attention from constructive criticism to prayerful use of the liturgy. One of the difficulties in any "new" liturgy is that it upsets old patterns of devotion. Most of us need help to establish new patterns. This session is a time to offer each other such help.

PURPOSE OF THIS SESSION

To help each other find ways more effectively to pray the liturgy.

PROCEDURE.

Point out that this is your last session together on this subject. If any feel they have been made too self-conscious about their worship, or that they have found the critical stance uncomfortable when they pray, admit that this seems to be an inevitable, if unpleasant, aspect of thoughtful reflection on liturgical change. We hope that we will become so aware of the meaning of the new that we will be able to take it for granted, like that old comfortable furniture we knew so well.

To move toward that direction, offer the following chart for silent study and reflection:

WHEN WE PRAY OUR LITURGY

An outline and some things to think about

- Entrance Rite

    All that precedes the Scripture readings is to bring the congregation together in the Lord's name and to prepare them to worship. Corporate song, greeting and response, corporate praise, and an opening prayer may all be used.

    How do these help us to become a worshiping community?

- Scripture Reading and Sermon

    The chief proclamation of the Word of God by the Church. Old Testament, Psalm, Epistle, and Gospel may be read followed by an interpretation of their meaning for today in the Sermon.

    How can I hear it better with the inward as well as outward ear?

- Prayer of the Faithful

    We pray for people in the Church and in the world.

    How can this prayer of intercession be my prayer, and *the prayer of the whole congregation,* and *the prayer of the Universal Church?*

Leader's Guide

- Confession of Sin

What would it mean for me to confess the sins of society as well as my own sin? To ask for forgiveness for my race or nation?

- The Peace

 To express our unity in the Body of Christ and our reconciliation with one another as we come to Eucharist together.

How can we use it to increase our sense of communion and community?

- The Offertory

 Bread, Wine. Money?

- The Great Thanksgiving

 The prayer of consecration is the central prayer of the Eucharist, said by the presiding priest in the name of the whole Church.

What is my part in the offering of the Church? In the offering of Christ? How can I best unite myself with Christ and the Church in this prayer?

- Breaking of Bread

 This symbolic and practical act is highlighted by silence.

What is being broken? What does the breaking mean?

- Communion

 We eat together.

Who are we communing with? Who are we in union with?

- Dismissal

 We are sent into the world to be the Church.

Is the Eucharist over for me? How could it continue?

When the group has had a few minutes to study the chart in silence, encourage members to talk about any question in the right-hand column that interests them. Since this is their last session together many may have things they want to say. Encourage them to move from the analytical mood to the prayerful mood.

Draw the discussion to a close by sharing any convictions you may have gained in the course of the study. Then call the group's attention to the final chapter (VI.) it should be helpful to those who wonder why we are making such a fuss about the liturgy when there are so many seemingly more important things that demand the Church's attention. Also note the list of Books for Further Reading, and add suggestions of your own.

If it seems appropriate, close the session with a silent prayer, a prayer of your own, one written by the group in an earlier session, or one of the litanies the group has studied and liked.

Books for Further Reading

Babin, David. *The Celebration of Life: Our Changing Liturgy.* New York: Morehouse-Barlow, 1969. (A good explanation of liturgical change from the point of view of the Liturgical Movement in the Episcopal Church.)

———.*Doing the Eucharist.* New York: Morehouse-Barlow, 1971. (A guide to the use of the trial liturgies of the Episcopal Church by an enthusiastic supporter.)

Bouyer, Louis. *The Liturgy Revived.* Notre Dame: University of Notre Dame Press, 1964. (A doctrinal commentary on the *Constitution on the Sacred Liturgy* by an outstanding Roman Catholic scholar.)

Champlin, Joseph. *Christ Present and Yet to Come.* Maryknoll, N.Y.: Orbis, 1971. (An approach to the celebration of the new Roman Catholic liturgy by a well-known liturgist, intended primarily for priests and members of parish worship committees.)

Micks, Marianne. *The Future Present.* New York: Seabury, 1970. (A serious study of what we do in Christian worship.)

Patino, J. *The New Order of Mass.* Collegeville, Minn.: Liturgical Press, 1970. (The Instruction of the new Roman Missal with a translation and commentary.)

Shands, Alfred R. *The Liturgical Movement and the Local Church.* New York: Morehouse-Barlow, 1965. (An attempt to set the renewal of worship in a wider context of parish life.)

Sloyan, Gerard. *Worship in a New Key.* New York: Herder, 1965. (A popular introduction to the liturgical changes stemming from Vatican Council II.)

Stevick, Daniel. *Language in Worship.* New York: Seabury, 1970. (Deals with the problem of the use of the English language in worship, a must for parish worship committees.)

White, James F. *New Forms of Worship.* Nashville: Abingdon, 1971. (A popularly written survey at what is happening in worship by an outstanding Methodist liturgical scholar.)

Additional Books Cited in the Background Reading

Authorized Services 1973. New York: Church Hymnal Corp., 1973.

Bouyer, Louis. *Liturgical Piety.* University of Notre Dame Press, 1955.

———. *Rite and Man.* University of Notre Dame Press, 1963.

Capon, Robert F. *An Offering of Uncles.* New York: Sheed and Ward, 1967.

Cellier, Frank S. *Liturgy Is Mission.* New York: Seabury, 1964.

Constitution on the Sacred Liturgy. Collegeville, Minn.: Liturgical Press, 1964.

Cox, Harvey. *The Secular City.* New York: Macmillan, 1965.

Dix, Gregory. *The Shape of the Liturgy.* 2nd ed. London: Dacre Press, 1945.

Early Christian Fathers (Library of Christian Classics 1). Ed. Cyril C. Richardson. Philadelphia: Westminster, 1953.

Hebert, A. Gabriel. *Liturgy and Society.* London: Faber and Faber, 1935.

Herder Correspondence (August, 1964).

Jungmann, Joseph. *The Mass of the Roman Rite.* 2 vols. New York: Benziger Bros., 1951–1955.

Kavanagh, Aidan, "A Relevant Liturgy," *The Way* 11 (1970).

Ladd, William P. *Prayer Book Interleaves.* New York: Seabury, 1957.

McLuhan, Marshall. *The Gutenberg Galaxy.* University of Toronto Press, 1962.

Mead, Margaret. *The Ritual Expressions of the Cosmic Sense.* Cincinnati: Forward Movement Publications, 1966.

Michenneau, G. *Revolution in a City Parish.* Westminster, Md.: Newman, 1949.

Parish Program for Liturgy and Mission. Madison, Wis.: Associated Parishes, 1963.

Sacramentary for Sundays and Other Occasions (Provisional Text). Washington: National Conference of Catholic Bishops, 1972.

Schmemann, Alexander. *For the Life of the World.* New York: National Student Christian Federation, 1963.

Services for Trial Use. New York: Church Hymnal Corp., 1971.

Shepherd, Massey. *The Liturgical Renewal of the Church.* New York: Oxford, 1960.

Spaight, Robert. "Liturgy and Language," *Theology* 74 (1972).

Teilhard de Chardin, Pierre. *Hymn of the Universe.* New York: Harper and Row, 1961.

The Liturgy of the Lord's Supper (Prayer Book Studies 17). New York: Church Hymnal Corp., 1966.

Underhill, Evelyn. *Worship.* London: Nisbet, 1936.

Vogel, Arthur. *Is the Last Supper Finished?* New York: Sheed and Ward, 1968.

Worship in Spirit and in Truth. Ed. Donald Garfield. Boston: Jarrow, 1970.